THE EXPRESS

BUYING YOUR FIRST FRANCHISE

The Express Guides

The Express and Kogan Page have joined forces to publish a series of practical guides offering no-nonsense advice on a wide range of financial, legal and business topics.

Whether you want to manage your money better, make more money, get a new business idea off the ground – and make sure it's legal – there's an Express Guide for you.

Titles published so far are:

Great Ideas for Making Money
Niki Chesworth

Your Money
How to Make the Most of it
(Second edition)
Niki Chesworth

Buying a Property Abroad
(Second edition)
Niki Chesworth

How to Sell More
A Guide for Small Business
(Second edition)
Neil Johnson

The Woman's Guide to Finance
How to Manage All Your Money Matters
(Second edition)
Tony Levene

Buying Your First Franchise
(Second edition)
G R Clarke

Investment Guide
Practical Advice for Making the Right Choice (Second edition)
Tony Levene

Network Marketing
An Introductory Guide
David Barber

How to Cope with Separation and Divorce (Second edition)
David Green

Your Home Office
A Practical Guide to Using Technology Successfully (Revised second edition)
Peter Chatterton

You and the Law
A Simple Guide to All Your Legal Problems (Second edition)
Susan Singleton

How to Cut Your Tax Bill Without Breaking the Law
(Fourth edition)
Grant Thornton, Chartered Accountants

Readymade Business Letters That Get Results (Second edition)
Jim Douglas

Be Your Own Boss
How to Set Up a Successful Small Business (Second edition)
David McMullan

Available from all good bookshops, or to obtain further information please contact the publishers at the address below:

Kogan Page Ltd
120 Pentonville Rd
London N1 9JN
Tel: 0171-278 0433
Fax: 0171-837 6348

THE EXPRESS

BUYING YOUR FIRST FRANCHISE

SECOND EDITION

GREG CLARKE

KOGAN PAGE

To
Charlotte Kathleen Bonnie

Kogan Page Limited, *The Express* and the author cannot assume legal responsibility for the accuracy of any particular statement in this work. No responsibility for loss or damage occasioned to any person acting or refraining from action as a result of material in this publication can be accepted by the authors or publishers.

First published in 1995
This edition published in 1997

Kogan Page Limited
120 Pentonville Road,
London N1 9JN

British Library Cataloguing in Publication Data

A CIP record for this book is available from the British Library.

ISBN 0-7494-2014-6

Typeset by Books Unlimited (Nottm), NG19 7BZ

Printed and bound in Great Britain by Clays Ltd, St Ives plc

Contents

Acknowledgements

My thanks go to the franchisees mentioned in the case studies, who each responded wholeheartedly and unreservedly to my questions and helped to make this book possible. I must thank their franchisors and many others for positively supporting my requests to approach their franchisees. It is indicative of the nature of modern ethical franchising that most franchisors whom I approached warmly welcomed the idea that their franchisees should be asked to discuss freely their own experiences. In this respect I also acknowledge the active assistance of Brian Smart, Director of the British Franchise Association, and wish to thank him and the BFA for the very positive support I received.

Likewise, I wish to thank John Burley Public Relations Consultants Ltd of Matlock, Derbyshire, for furnishing me with full details of the finalists of the 1996 and 1997 British Franchise Association's Awards, which are sponsored by Midland Bank and *The Express* and which they organise.

My thanks go to all those within the field of franchising who have helped me over the years to develop my knowledge and understanding of the subject, the companies, and the people involved with them. In particular I am grateful to Mike Matthews of FMM Ltd and Andrew James.

I would also like to mention John Pratt of solicitors Pinsent & Co, Lynne Lister of *Business Franchise* magazine, Bob and Nick Riding of *Franchise World* magazine, Peter Stern of National Westminster Bank plc, the managers within the franchise units of Lloyds Bank, Midland Bank and the Royal Bank of Scotland, and those formerly within the franchise unit of Barclays Bank.

I am indebted to Wendy Gill of Keyworth Typing Services, who unflinchingly helped to produce the manuscript for the first edition of this book, as well as those for my previous books and mini-guides, when I have run right up to deadline! I am also grateful for her help and advice in keeping my new word processor and printer working properly to produce this second edition of *Buying Your First Franchise*.

FUTURESHAPE

A beautiful franchise opportunity

Satisfying the demands of the continually growing health industry, a Futureshape franchise now offers a comprehensive package that provides a range of head to toe treatments. The beauty of this franchise lies in its great adaptability. You need not be a qualified therapist nor a doctor to be a franchisee. Simply having the vision to see the potential this franchise offers will enable you to lay the foundations on which to build a multi faceted health and beauty business.

By creating a niche market position, thereby overcoming the shortfalls of normal salons, Futureshape have developed and patented a diverse range of body treatments that target the ABC1 income bracket.

Medi-Cell, the top of the range treatment is, designed to combat cellulite, a condition that effects over 90% of women. Be they slim, fat, rich, famous or the girl next door, cellulite knows no bounds. Medi-Cell attacks cellulite at precisely the right depth and frequency deep within the body tissue by means of uniquely calibrated ultrasound waves. These enable the clusters of mineral deposits to be broken-up and massaged away through the lymphatic system. The unique aspect lies in the ability to detect the embedded cellulite clusters, using Medi-Scan, a thermoencapsulated heat detector. This gives an 'x-ray' of the cellulite. One session of Medi-Cell lasts around an hour and offers an effective non-invasive alternative to painful treatments such as liposuction.

Weight-loss is an ongoing concern for both sexes. Medi-Slim was developed to address this very problem. Using the scientific principle of thermogenesis, a gel is applied to the body in order to lower the body temperature. This in turn encourages a fat burning process, which converts natural fat reserves into energy. As a result the excess kilos fall away and in many cases dramatic weight-loss has been known to occur. This is a very simple yet easy method of overcoming weight concern. What you have with Medi-Slim is not only a wide customer base with a method that does not require stringent diets but also can be targeted to reduce specific fat pockets, yet is based on the body's natural phenomena.

Medi-Tone is a state-of-the-art electronic muscle stimulator. Top models such as Cindy Crawford are known to favour this method of toning and exercising. With a range of diverse applications such as toning slack tissue, fat burning or breast enhancement, a session on this simple to operate machine can equate to three hours in the gym! Fortunately clients do not have to put in hours of strenuous exercise but simply lie on a couch whilst pads strapped to the body are programmed to carry out the treatment you require. It is not only used as an individual treatment, but also to enhance or compliment the aforementioned treatments - Medi-Cell and Medi-Slim.

Very much in vogue at the moment is pneumotherapy. This is a process in which sequentially inflated air chambers in the shape of boots that cover the stomach and legs down to the ankles, are designed to give a deep, relaxing lymphatic massage. Medi-Shape can therefore treat diverse conditions such as water retention and sports injuries, detoxifying the limbs and reshaping.

The least time consuming treatment within the portfolio is the Medi-Lift non-surgical treatment which works on toning tired and wrinkled facial tissue. Using micro electrical currents, pads placed on specific areas combine to contract muscles on the face, thus stimulating and strengthening them to give immediate and long lasting results. Thus this ten minute treatment can effectively provide a quick turn-over of customers and revenue.

To provide even further cash, a centre can capitalise on its customer base by selling the range of natural food supplements and beauty products especially developed to compliment the treatments. These products include the ground breaking Fat Magnets and Shrinkers.

It is worth nothing that consultations and diagnosis for any of the treatments are completely free, hence encouraging potential clients to gauge the suitability of them without any obligation.

No wonder then that since their first franchise was sold in 1994, Futureshape have built up an impressive array of 150 clinics in over 33 countries. Franchisees include individuals who have started from rented premises and expanded, to a friend of Arnold Shwarzenneggar who has built up a chain of Futureshape clinics within fitness centres in Austria.

A Complete Futureshape International Franchise cost £29,950, which includes all the equipment, start-up cosmetics, training in London, protected territory based on post codes, point of sale material, support and advertising bromides needed.

futureshape

..... Futureprofit

Don't look for the ordinary - *look for the extraordinary!*

Without doubt, the health and beauty industry has been the boom industry in the last decade. Alternative therapies have seen a surgence of interest creating another huge market place - Futureshape have seen a niche in this lucrative industry.

Cellulite is a condition that affects 90% of women, whatever their age. Weight-loss for both Men and Women is an area in which there is a constant demand. Natural non-invasive methods developed by the companys doctors have enabled Futureshape to become the undisputed leader.

With a low cost start up and package that includes equipment, training, protected territory, advertising bromides and point of sale material. Futureshape are actively recruiting franchises, including Master licences for territories Worldwide.

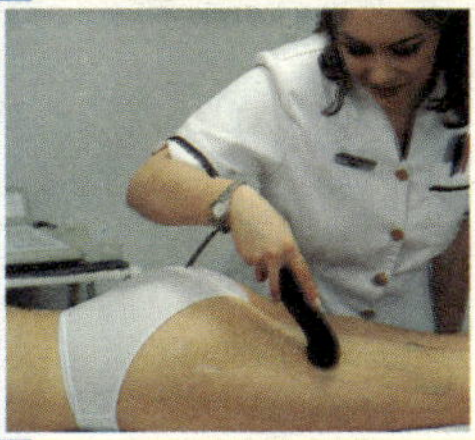

CENTRES IN:-
AUSTRALIA, AUSTRIA, BELGIUM, CZECH REP, DUBAI, INDIA, IRELAND, KUWAIT, NETHERLANDS, SAUDI ARABIA, SINGAPORE, SOUTH AFRICA, TURKEY & UKRAINE.

Telephone our London office in order to arrange a visit to our owner operated clinic, get a feel for the business and ask us any questions that you have on your mind.

Futureshape International Ltd,
34 Sloane Avenue, London SW3 3AX.
Tel: 0171 584 6515.
Fax: 0171 589 1455
for further information.

Now in 147 centres worldwide

1
Introduction

Taking up a franchise means being self-employed. No form of self-employment is without risk. However, risk can be assessed and controlled by identifying and minimising the main risk factors.

Risks lie in launching a business, sustaining it and building it. The natural state of any business is to go bust. It has been said that one way to become the owner of a small business is to buy a large one – and simply wait a year!

To become successfully self-employed, you will first need to identify the existence of two essentials: a market, and a viable route to that market. That is, customers and profitable ways of reaching them and doing business with them. Without customers, you do not have a business, but they can be elusive, and even when you have found them they can be fickle. Franchising is now recognised as an often highly successful way of doing business because, along with its other attractions, it deals with those two essentials. Whether you are buying a franchise which is new to the area of your choice, or buying one that has already been established by someone else, you are buying the right to tread a proven path with a guide to show you the way.

This book seeks to assist you in your decision-making as you proceed to buy your first franchise. It may also help you to decide whether taking up a franchise is indeed the right path for you.

To help you to visualise your own future, a wide range of case studies is included. These give examples of a variety of personal backgrounds, types of business, location and experience. The case studies have not been selected simply to show franchising in a good light. They are all real histories and to the best of the author's knowledge the named franchisees are still trading as described.

The final chapter lists sources of further information and advice. You would be wise to follow these up as your next step. Before signing any contract or agreement and before allocating any money to a particular venture, you are strongly recommended to take professional legal and financial advice, preferably from a solicitor who is experienced in franchising and an accountant with experience in the field of your choice.

2

What's in a name?

This guide introduces you to the concept and language of franchising, and provides some background information about franchising in the UK as a whole.

The word 'franchise' is used rather loosely in a number of different contexts, but generally it is understood to mean that a right has been accorded for some specified purpose. For example, it can mean the right to vote. In a business context, the word can describe the right to broadcast commercial television or radio, or to carry out certain operations under licence, for example the bottling and canning of soft drinks.

It is also used to describe the subject of this book, although in this case it is more correctly termed 'business format franchising' and is the way in which such well-known business names as McDonald's and the Body Shop have chosen to develop.

Business format franchising

Business format franchising is the type of business arrangement in which one party (the franchisor) grants a licence to another individual, partnership, or company (the franchisee) which gives the right to trade under the trade mark and business name of the franchisor. It includes the knowledge and use of the franchisor's trade secrets and all the elements necessary to establish a previously untrained person in their own legally separate business, running it with continuing advice and support on a predetermined basis and for a specified period of time. In return, the franchisee pays initial and ongoing fees and agrees to be bound by the terms of the franchise agreement, running his or her business strictly in accordance with the systems and procedures laid down in the franchisor's operations manual.

Through business format franchising the franchisor offers the franchisee a blueprint of a successful business. The product range or service and all operational aspects should have been thoroughly market tested in pilot operations run by the franchisor. The franchise 'package' should thus contain a complete business format that has been tried, tested, and proven. As well as including the right to produce or sell goods or services under an established trade mark or business name, it should also provide the following:

- A detailed product and/or service specification;
- Operating systems and manuals;
- Training and help to establish the business;
- Business style, logo, colours;
- Accounting and financial systems;
- Marketing, public relations and advertising support;
- Ongoing research and development for products/services;
- Ongoing research, analysis and interpretation of market intelligence and the communication of trends;
- Provision for up-dating skills training in line with the changing needs of the business;
- Continuing advice and support.

When a number of franchisees are established, a network is created comprised of like-minded investing individuals, each running the business in their own location. Each franchisee operates within the franchisor's corporate image, offering customers consistency in products and/or service. Consistency, day in, day out, from every location in the network, is expected by today's customer. The success of all the well-known chain stores and national service providers can be largely attributed to the achievement of consistency in their delivery and service to the customer.

In each case, the business format franchise is a comprehensive and continuing relationship in which the initial concept is perpetually being developed. The resources available for such development are contributed by the franchisor and all franchisees, and are therefore much greater than any one individual could reasonably afford or command. Business format franchises can therefore be distinguished from other types of marketing/business arrangements and should be assessed accordingly.

Other types of business franchise

Lease franchise. This is where the 'parent' company leases premises to the self-employed operator for rental payments based on turnover and including a management services fee. This is similar to a landlord/tenant agreement.

Master licence. Franchisors can sell the right to operate their systems in another country. The master licensee/franchisee can then sell franchises in that country in the usual way and will remit a proportion of the royalties from his or her franchisees abroad to the parent franchisor. The master licence operation might also be a joint venture between the parent franchisor and the master licensee where both have invested capital and both share in the profits.

Soft franchise. This term is used to describe a type of profit-sharing arrangement where the 'franchisee' (often a branch manager) takes a proportion of the profit without having to make a cash investment in the business. Responsibility for some of the running costs of the unit is passed to the 'franchisee', who can therefore directly influence profit. For an absent business owner, it also neatly transfers responsibility for stock and cash to a motivated and committed local manager without allowing any other rights.

Sub-franchise. These are franchises granted within the territory of an existing franchisee, who may be termed an *area franchisee*. The resulting tiered structure could be illegal under the UK pyramid selling laws and therefore such agreements are usually structured and worded very carefully.

System leasing. Coined by Moshe Gerstenhaber of Kall-Kwik Ltd, this is another way of describing business format franchising. Here, the franchisor leases to the franchisee a proven business system for a specified period in return for up-front and ongoing fees.

Alternative arrangements that may be offered by a 'parent' company include: various kinds of agency; an operating licence; a distributorship or dealership; multi-level (or network) marketing; and a joint venture or marketing alliance. A guide to such options within self-employment is *Ready-made Business Opportunities* by the author and published by Kogan Page.

The franchise industry in the 1990s

The thirteenth annual survey conducted on behalf of the British Franchise Association and published in March 1997 carries the note, 'If franchising is considered in its broader context and tenanted pubs, petrol stations, car dealerships and soft drink bottlers are included, it is estimated that the total market is worth £33.3 billion. It is estimated that franchising now accounts for 19 per cent of all retail sales which, in comparison to the United States where the comparable figure is around 35 per cent, gives it plenty of scope for continued expansion.'

The 1997 survey reported that overall turnover through business format franchising in the UK had risen to £6.4 billion. The number of franchise systems has increased by 30 per cent since 1994 and there are now 541 businesses choosing business format franchising for their development, supporting 26,800 individual franchised units, which themselves are growing to give total employment in the sector of 264,000.

Peter Stern, Head of NatWest UK's Franchise Section, commented, 'It is good to see continuing development in all areas of franchising in the UK, notably 94 per cent of franchisees reporting profitability – the highest figure recorded since our Surveys began in 1984. Also, franchisees' satisfaction is at an all time high with 92 per cent saying that they were satisfied with their franchisor relationship. Furthermore, 95 per cent of franchisors believe that this year will realise even better prospects for their business – again the highest figure yet recorded.' As Brian Smart, Director-General of the British Franchise Association points out, 'Franchising has proved to be the most successful way of starting a new business.'

According to the Survey, age is becoming less of an issue if you are looking to invest in a franchise, and is certainly not a barrier, as it attracts people of all ages. Of those franchisees surveyed, 41 per cent were aged under 40. There have been increases in the number under 30 years old, and between 41 and 50 years old. One in ten franchisees are under 30, and one in five are over 50. Asking the franchisors what they are looking for, 75 per cent do not specify an age preference – compared to 49 per cent in 1993.

Also, 23 per cent of those surveyed were single. The majority were men, although the number of female franchisees has risen to 27 per cent. 85 per cent of the franchisors do not specify whether they are looking for a man or a woman, or if they would rather they were married. For most businesses there is no requirement for previous experience or qualifications in that industry.

The Survey goes on to report, 'For the fourth consecutive year the average length of time a franchise system has been operating has increased. In 1992 the figure was 6.2 years but it has now risen to 7.9 years. This figure continues to indicate the growing maturity of many franchises despite a significant increase in the number of franchise systems identified in the past two years.

While franchising as a concept is nationwide, regional representation varies and this looks set to continue. Franchising remains strongest in London, the South East, the South West, the West Midlands and the North West. Franchising is also an increasingly powerful method of expanding a business internationally. Already 26 per cent of the UK's franchised businesses claim to operate in other European countries and 49 per cent plan to be in mainland Europe by the year 2000.'

Franchise contracts are often arranged for terms of five or ten years and generally contain reasonable clauses for renewal. Previous surveys have shown that of those contracts due for renewal in the 12 months prior to the survey, nearly all are renewed. It is also generally estimated that around 45 per cent of all franchisees have previously been self-employed, while 55 per cent have never previously run their own business.

Copies of the survey are available, priced £77.50, from the British Franchise Association (address given in Chapter 10).

Industry indications are that possibly half the people taking up a franchise would not have become self-employed were it not for the franchise format. Also, that the ability of franchising to assist would-be small-business people to make the transition from employee to entrepreneur is one of the major reasons for its increasing popularity.

The advantages of franchising

A properly run and proven franchise will almost certainly be a less risky, more straightforward and structured way of going into business than setting up independently. This is because in a good franchise:

- The business concept and existence of a market have been proved.
- The ways to approach that market and operate the business profitably have already been worked out and tested.
- The know-how is passed on to the franchisee through initial and ongoing training, advice, guidance and support. Specialised knowledge in the proposed business activity is therefore not a prerequisite for the prospective franchisee.
- The franchisor should provide ongoing market intelligence, being in a position to monitor and analyse trends, opportunities and threats to the business. The franchisor is therefore better placed than the individual operator to determine the overall strategic direction of the business.

The risks of business failure are thus substantially reduced. Other business advantages can also be attained.

- Finance may be more readily available to franchisees than to those setting up on their own, because of the proven success of franchising and track record of the franchisor.
- The lead-time in making the franchise business successful may be reduced as franchisees have the immediate use of an established name and the reputation already built up by the franchisor.
- Franchisees are able to make use of the franchisor's purchasing power, and there may be benefits arising from the size of the network operations.
- Regional and national advertising and promotion may be afforded and undertaken.
- Franchisees may receive territorial protection.
- Retail franchises may have the benefit of the franchisor's strength of covenant, to help obtain leasehold premises in prime locations.
- Franchisees are the owners of their own businesses (although restrictions are imposed by their franchise agreements).

Being part of a franchise network offers the further advantage of being in contact with like-minded individuals who are 'friends' in the same business. This may be of particular comfort if you have a need for companionship in your endeavours, and can help to alleviate a feeling of being out on your own.

Of course, franchisors also benefit by the arrangements. They can generally expand their trade name and activities more quickly through investment from franchisees than solely through their own resources. They too will gain by the increased purchasing power for their own activities, while passing on responsibility for cash and stock security in each 'branch' to the local franchisee. Above all, the franchisor wins local commitment to the business and its customers from the investing franchisee.

The disadvantages of franchising

If the franchisor's business and its franchise operations are not correctly structured and ethically managed, the franchisee may not gain the benefits of franchising. Other aspects to be considered are:

- A franchise is subject to substantial control from the franchisor.
- An initial fee is payable to the franchisor, adding to the amount of start-up capital required before launching a new business.

- Ongoing management services fees or royalties are payable to the franchisor; the business must be able to support these and continue to be profitable for the franchisee.
- Restrictions may be placed on the franchisee's ability to sell the franchise, or to pass it to a relative. It is usual for the franchisor to insist on assessing the proposed buyer's suitability and apply its normal selection criteria before approving a transfer of ownership. Further, the franchisor may require a substantial payment should the franchise ownership be transferred. Franchises cannot normally be assigned.
- The franchisee's business may be adversely affected by the actions of the other franchisees and operations will be directly affected by the actions, or insolvency, of the franchisor.

Of course, the franchisor too faces uncertainties, particularly in divulging its business know-how and entrusting its business name and reputation to others.

Types, range, and scope of business format franchise

A variety of business types exists within the broad definition of business format franchising. An attempt is made here to categorise them, although in practice you will find that franchises often fit into several categories.

Job franchise. A 'one person' business where the owner is normally the operator of the franchise, sometimes run from his or her home. This type of franchise usually offers a mobile or van-based service to local customers, who may be other businesses and/or the general public.

Distribution franchise. Often arises when a company employs delivery drivers or roundspeople to distribute its products and then allows such employees to buy out and operate their rounds on a self-employed basis, selling only those goods that are approved by the franchisor. New franchisees may be recruited directly on these terms and franchisees may be permitted to operate multiple rounds by employing their own staff. The business will generally operate out of a depot owned and run by the franchisor or by a depot (regional) franchisee servicing a number of distribution franchisees Customers may be other businesses and/or the public.

Depot franchise. The franchisee operates a depot-based business servicing trade and/or retail customers. The business may also include a sale counter on the premises and/or a fleet of distribution vehicles, which are either owned directly by the depot franchisee or by distributors or sub-franchisees.

Retail franchise. Franchisees are required to open retail outlets to display and sell products approved by the franchisor. The franchisee will generally employ staff to serve customers on the premises and, if warranted, the outlet may be run on a day-to-day basis by management employed by the franchisee.

Investment franchise. For particularly large business operations involving substantial capital expenditure, the franchisee as investor will normally employ a management team and staff and may have little or no active involvement in the day-to-day running of the business.

There are a few customer-based businesses that cannot lend themselves to franchising. With over 540 franchisors in the UK, operating through 26,800 outlets, there are plenty from which to choose – often several competing against each other in the same market.

Many well-known business names (and many not well-known) are operated through franchises. Broad details of each can be found in editorials and advertisements in a number of publications and directories (see Chapter 10).

An idea of the range of business activities that have been franchised, together with a selection of the more widely known companies involved is given below. These are examples only: inclusion in the list is not to be taken as a recommendation, nor should exclusion of a particular company be interpreted adversely.

Building and Property Services	Decorating Den, Dyno-Locks, Dyno-Rod, Gun-Point, Metro Rod, Mixamate Concrete.
Business Services	Minster Services, Pitman Training, Signs Express, Sketchley, Recognition Express, Swinton.
Cleaning Services	Chem-Dry, Molly Maid, Rainbow International, Safeclean, ServiceMaster, Vendo Plc.
Computer Services	Ribbon Revival, Techclean.
Distribution Services	Amtrak, City Link, Dairy Crest, Dale Farm, Durex Vending, Interlink Express, Motabitz, Panic Link, Red Star Parcels, Securicor Pony Express, Trust Parts, Unigate Dairies.

Employment Agencies/Training	Alfred Marks, BSM, Driver Hire, Humana International, Travail.
Estate Services	Legal & General, Seekers.
Fast Print	Alphagraphics, Kall-Kwik, PDC Copyprint, Prontaprint.
Food & Drink	Alpine Soft Drinks, Burger King, Domino's Pizza, Greenalls Inn Partnership, Häagen-Dazs, Harry Ramsden's, KFC, McDonald's, Perfect Pizza, Pierre Victoire, Spudulike, Wimpy.
Greeting Cards	Card Connection.
Health & Beauty	Rosemary Conley, Saks, The Tanning Shop.
Motoring Services	Autela, Budget Rent A Car, Mr Clutch, Computa Tune, Hertz UK, Highway Glass, Hometune, MAC Tools, Snap-On-Tools.
Nursing & Home Care	CareConnect Home Services, Carewatch, Everycare.
Professional Services	Just Wills, Nationwide Investigations, Pirtek.
Specialised	Auto-Smart, Cupboard Love, Hospital Entertainment, Kwik Strip, Snappy Snaps.
Travel & Accommodation	Uniglobe Travel, Holiday Inns.
Walk in Retail	Alldays, Applewoods, The Body Shop, Clarks, Dolland & Aitchison, Durham Pine, Esso, In-toto Kitchens, The Levi Shop, Mobile Phone Centre, Nevada Bob, Post Office Counters, Thorntons, Vantage Pharmacy.

3
Legal aspects

A rudimentary knowledge of the law is needed by anyone running their own business; ignorance of the law is not a defence against criminal proceedings. Likewise, the legal maxim of 'let the buyer beware' (*caveat emptor*) applies as much to taking up a franchise as any other transaction not specifically covered by, for example, consumer law.

There is no single law or specific Act of Parliament controlling franchising in the UK. However, the fundamentals are governed by the range of laws and precedents that already exists within Britain and the European Union. For example, contract law plays an important role and the various UK competition laws have to be taken into consideration by any franchisor setting up a franchise system. Likewise, there exist EU competition laws that are generally embodied in Article 85 of the Treaty of Rome. Even so, the EU has introduced a block exemption regulation that exempts properly constructed franchise agreements from EU competition law, subject to compliance with the conditions in the regulation.

It is beyond the scope of this book to cover all the legal aspects of franchising in detail. Apart from the overall framework of law within which franchising operates, each franchising company will have its own way of doing business and a unique contract constructed specifically to suit its own needs and that of its business. Any prospective franchisee is therefore strongly urged to obtain independent legal advice, preferably from a solicitor experienced in franchising law, before signing any contract or agreement and before committing funds. A current listing of solicitors who are affiliated to the British Franchise Association (BFA) may be obtained directly from the BFA, or from one of the franchise directories (see Chapter 10).

In all successful franchise systems an essential ingredient is the special business relationship that exists between franchisor and franchisee. That relationship should be built on trust arising from mutual respect for each other's role in developing the business. However, from the outset those roles need to be clearly defined within a framework that will allow the relationship to form and flourish. At the same time, the framework should be able to deal with departures by either party from the original joint aspirations, as well as allowing for its termination. Promises from either side must be translated with integrity into tangible actions and suitable provisions agreed to cover all eventualities.

The franchise agreement

To record accurately the full nature, extent and limitations of the deal that the franchisor offers the franchisee, together with details of what is expected from the franchisee in return, it is essential that both parties commit themselves to a binding agreement. The franchise agreement is a written and signed, legally binding contract between franchisor and franchisee. It sets out the rights and obligations of each party and contains provisions for certain eventualities, as well as procedures for dealing with unforeseen circumstances. Whether it is termed an 'agreement', 'contract' or 'licence', it is the document by which the franchisor ultimately controls each franchisee in the network.

The franchise agreement is not usually negotiable, since the franchisor cannot claim to operate a coherent network if many variations of the contract exist. Franchisees should have no cause to believe that they have in any way been disadvantaged by the franchisor if they compare their own franchise agreement with those of other franchisees in the network.

Although you will not be able to alter the terms of the franchise agreement, the advice of a qualified solicitor should still be sought to find out, in layman's terms, exactly what the implications are of each clause. Importantly, an experienced franchise solicitor will be able to spot significant omissions from the contract. The document is often lengthy and you will need a thorough working knowledge of its entire contents if you are to legally commit yourself, your funds, and your business efforts. If you were to become embroiled in a serious dispute with your franchisor over the terms of your agreement, you might find you had no recourse in law if it considered you were foolhardy or reckless in having signed the contract in the first place.

Clauses in the agreement that appear onerous at first sight are often designed to protect the franchisee's business interests, just as they are the franchisor's. All operations in the network are subject to the same quality standards, scrutiny and guidance from the franchisor in order to protect consistency of delivery to the customer, and the reputation on which the success of the business is founded.

Key clauses in a franchise agreement

There is no such thing as a standard franchise agreement, although each contract should of course give details of any defined operating territory. It is also likely to contain certain key clauses as shown below.

This franchise agreement is made between ______________Ltd and its associate companies whose registered offices are at ______________ as specified in Part 1 of the Schedule hereto and their successors and assignees (hereinafter called 'the Franchisor') of the One Part and ______________________ the person, firm or company specified in Part 2 of the said Schedule (hereinafter called 'the Franchisee') of the Other Part.

---

1. Recitals
2. Rights granted
3. Term of agreement/licence
4. Rights of renewal
5. The Franchisor's initial obligations
6. The Franchisor's obligations
7. The Franchisee's obligations
8. Training
9. Improvements
10. Licence fee and management service fee/royalty
11. Accountancy
12. Advertising
13. Insurance
14. Sale of business
15. Non-competition
16. Death of principal
17. Termination
18. Consequences of termination
19. Failure to exercise rights not to be waived
20. Franchisor's right of set-off
21. Indemnification of franchisor by the franchisee
22. Severability
23. Acknowledgement to advice given
24. Further acknowledgements

25. Warranties without authority
26. Principal's guarantee
27. Arbitration
28. Notices
29. Terms of purchase of the said products

A franchisee may trade as a sole trader, a partnership, or a limited liability company. The franchise agreement must be constructed according to each type of business status, although in practice your chosen franchisor may prefer that you do not operate as a limited liability company. This is because the innate strength of most franchise systems is the personal involvement, investment and commitment from the individuals with whom the franchisor has chosen to sustain an ongoing business relationship. For the same reason, those franchisors who do not object to the franchisee being a limited liability company, or even prefer that status, will generally not permit any transfer or other dealing in the shares of the franchisee company without its prior written approval.

Whatever your trading status, you will not be permitted to assign the franchise to anyone else. That is, you would be able to sell outright to a purchaser approved by the franchisor, but not sub-franchise or otherwise introduce a new principal into the business who is not named in the franchise agreement.

Sole traders are personally liable for all debts of the business. Partners are each equally and severally liable for all debts. This means that if your partner runs up debts on the business, even without your knowledge, then you will be equally liable for their repayment if you have any assets that can be seized. A limited liability company is a business that has a separate legal identity to its founders and shareholders. Their liability for the company's debts is limited to the amount (usually none) unpaid on the shares they own, unless of course they have given personal guarantees to lenders such as banks.

To help you decide which trading status would be best suited to your needs and personal circumstances it is advisable to consult an experienced accountant as well as your solicitor.

Premises

One of the most important, potentially stressful and high-risk aspects of any business can be finding the right premises from which to operate. The legalities alone can be a minefield for the unwary and independent assistance from an experienced solicitor is again strongly recommended. Leases may prove too short, too long or too demanding in their rent review or renewal clauses. Taking on a full repairing and insuring lease requires very careful consideration of the existing condition of the property and the financial commitment involved. Buying freehold (if available) may mean that you are entering the property business, in terms of investment and risk.

If your proposed franchise business requires premises, your franchisor should be able to advise on the size, type and location best suited to your needs. The amount of involvement the franchisor has in finding and arranging the right premises varies, but in most cases the franchisor will reserve the right of approval.

For a franchise that is heavily dependent on suitable premises, such as a retail operation, the franchisor may take the head-lease (or freehold) and grant you an under-lease. The arrangements for you to lease the premises would be drawn up 'back-to-back' with the franchise agreement: that is, both contracts run in tandem with each other to cover the same term. This can be an ideal arrangement since you can 'plug into' the franchise, the premises and the whole business system for the specified period and 'plug out' again when the contract terminates.

Equally, the franchisor retains the location for continuity of trading. In practice, as a new business person just starting up, you may have no choice but to rely on the franchisor's strength of covenant to obtain a particularly attractive site. This aspect is one of the benefits of joining forces with a franchisor that is a larger, established company.

Just as the franchisor may wish to retain title to premises to ensure business continuity, the same will generally apply to telephone and fax numbers, although you will be obliged to pay the running costs incurred by your business.

Signing an option or purchase agreement

If you wish to secure a particular franchise territory but are not ready to start trading, you may be offered an option to purchase. In this case you will be required to pay a deposit, usually deductible from the purchase price of the franchise, and be asked to sign a purchase agreement. This legal contract will have a time limit, usually a year, and is often employed when premises are to be sought and brought into use before trading can commence. Failure to progress substantially towards the start of trading within the time can mean forfeiting the deposit.

Confidentiality agreement

Since franchisors are offering 'know-how' and insights into their otherwise secret procedures, any prospective franchisee may be asked to sign a confidentiality agreement before in-depth discussions about the business can proceed. This is understandable and does not place you under any other obligation. Indeed, should you eventually take up the franchise you will be reassured to know that information for which you have paid is not freely available to others who are not likewise bound. As the franchise agreement of each existing franchisee will also contain a stringent confidentiality clause, any of the existing franchisees could place themselves in breach of their contract by talking to you about their experience, unless you too are legally obliged to maintain confidentiality.

The operations manual

The operations manual, or operating manual, is a complete description of all the operating policies, procedures, methods and systems used to run the business. It is by adherence to this common point of reference that all franchisees and the franchisor's own outlets can work consistently day by day and coherently as a network. It is a quality assurance guide, a training manual, an *aide mémoire* and reference book. The details it contains are essential for success in following the franchisor's proven route to the market.

Whereas the franchise agreement remains fixed and constant throughout the term of the franchise, the contents of the operations manual must be regularly up-dated by the franchisor as business methods change and evolve. For this reason it is usually presented in loose-leaf format, purposely written so as to be unambiguous, easy to read and easy to use.

By signing the franchise agreement, you are agreeing to adhere to the operations manual, even though you probably will not yet have been allowed to see its contents. You will also be promising to adhere to any future changes in the manual that the franchisor deems necessary. It should be noted that this ought not to provide a means by which the franchisor can make material changes to the agreement without your express permission. However, most amendments are in some way likely to affect your original business plan.

The operations manual invariably remains the property of the franchisor and must be surrendered on termination of the franchise agreement.

Arbitration

A well-structured franchise agreement will generally set out procedures to be adopted in the event of a dispute between franchisee and franchisor. The adoption of such provisions can be invaluable for resolving a dispute without prolonged acrimony, possibly allowing the franchisee/franchisor relationship to continue constructively and the franchise arrangement to otherwise run its course.

The BFA has such a scheme, administered by the Chartered Institute of Arbitrators. Under the scheme, it is only the franchisee who can elect to refer the dispute to arbitration, and even if the decision goes in favour of the franchisor, the franchisee pays only a third of the costs incurred, with the franchisor obliged to cover the remaining two-thirds. Such costs would be made up of the arbitrator's fee and the legal costs of both parties (the scheme incorporates measures to ensure these costs are not excessive). The franchisee would, however, have to pay any award granted to the franchisor for, say, damages arising out of the franchisee's breach of contract.

Selling or buying an existing franchise

Existing franchises can generally be bought and sold just as any other business. The difference is that the franchisor must be involved as a third party and the sale will not proceed without the franchisor's written approval. It is common, however, for the relevant clause in the franchise agreement to state that such approval is not to be unreasonably withheld by the franchisor.

The main requirement will be that the incoming franchisee meets the franchisor's usual standards of selection. The franchisor must also be satisfied that the proposed purchaser is exploring the franchise in good faith and not acquiring information to become a competitor. Even so, you would still be legally bound by the confidentiality clause in your franchise agreement.

In the event of your wishing to sell your franchise on, the franchisor may want first refusal to purchase (at the market price). Since the franchisor can claim to have been instrumental in developing the franchise with you, a proportion of the sale price including goodwill can be demanded by the franchisor. The exact details of a possible sale will be in your franchise agreement and, as with all other clauses, it is important to be aware from the outset precisely what those arrangements are.

If you are considering buying an existing franchise, the outgoing franchisee will be legally bound by conditions of sale in the franchise agreement as described above. As a prospective buyer, you will have to satisfy the franchisor's normal selection criteria and will be bound to abide by the usual rules of confidentiality.

In other respects, the legal aspects of buying an existing franchise are much the same as for the purchase of any other business that is up and running.

4

Financial aspects

Your franchisor should train you in the accounting systems and procedures to be used in the daily management and control of your franchise. These will also enable you regularly to report your sales figures and any necessary supporting information to your franchisor for calculation of ongoing fees that may be due. Such reporting will allow your franchisor to feed back to you comparative analyses of your franchise in the network. This can provide a very useful service for helping to identify trends in the market as well as in your own performance.

However, responsibility for the financial health of your business will rest with you. Whatever your business, getting the finances right from the start and continuing to control them is absolutely crucial for survival. You will be expected to have a firm grasp of all the financial aspects of your business, and to demonstrate commercial astuteness in your dealings.

Some of the advantages that running a franchise can offer over being a totally independent business are directly to do with the financial aspects, listed on pages 25-26. However, there are financial costs to be considered:

- An initial fee is payable to the franchisor, adding to the amount of start-up capital required before launching a new business.
- Ongoing management services fees or royalties are payable to the franchisor; the business must be capable of supporting these and remain suitably profitable for the franchisee.
- The franchisor may require a substantial payment should the franchise ownership be transferred.

Financial terms used in franchising

Initial fee. This includes the cost of buying the right to use the trading name, the provision of operating manuals and initial training for the franchisee. It helps the franchisor to recover the cost of franchisee recruitment and development of the franchise package. Often the initial fee covers some of the costs of helping to launch the franchisee's business. In effect, this is returned to the franchisee in the form of initial extra marketing support, opening stock or equipment.

NB. The initial fee comprises only one element of the total initial cost faced by the franchisee. Other costs may include shopfitting, equipment, software, communications and other services, stock, transport, accountancy and legal charges, as well as the financing of working capital to be employed in the business.

Management services fee. This is an ongoing fee, usually calculated as a percentage of the franchisee's gross sales net of VAT. It is normally paid weekly or monthly to the franchisor in return for continuing management services, advice, guidance, training and support.

Low services fees are not necessarily an advantage to the franchisee. It is crucial that the franchisor retains an ongoing interest in the viability and development of the franchise. Promotion and development of the business format can only be achieved by the franchisor from continuing payment by franchisees. However, it must be noted that if the costs of the enterprise to the franchisee prove higher than forecast, paying the services fee could be a heavy burden for the franchisee's business.

The size of the services fee should be closely scrutinised, because it is based on sales, not profits. For example, if the franchisee's total costs are 70 per cent of the sales value, a service fee of 10 per cent represents one third of the profit. It is quite usual for the management services fee to represent between one-quarter and a one-third of the net contribution from the business. This may seem high, but remember that the sales figures achieved are in many cases far in excess of those reached by independent traders.

The management services fee is sometimes charged as a fixed amount to be paid weekly or monthly. This arrangement can act as an incentive for the franchisee at least to reach and sustain the target sales needed to cover the fee, but it can be extremely onerous if such targets are not met. The franchisee could be required to pay the fee irrespective of whether there is cash to do so. If the franchisee believes that failure to achieve the necessary target is due to an occurrence beyond his or her control, a dispute will certainly arise.

Royalties. Confusingly, this term is often used synonymously with 'management services fee'. A royalty is generally considered as financial recognition of the true ownership of the brand name by which the product or service is sold or of the intellectual property rights involved. Royalties are usually calculated as a percentage of turnover or may be a fixed sum charged on each unit sold.

Mark-up. It is also necessary to take into consideration what mark-ups, if any, are made by the franchisor on products or equipment supplied.

Where the franchisor is the exclusive supplier of the products used in the franchisee's business, the management services fee may be included in the price paid for the goods by the franchisee. The franchisor may claim that no royalties are payable and they may indeed not be separately listed on the invoice, but a percentage mark up figure will probably have been calculated by the franchisor to add to the normal manufacturing margin.

One apparent advantage of grouping together charges in this way can be that buying in greater bulk can mean bigger discounts and cheaper supplies. This should also apply to franchisees, where supplies are often an important part of the cost of the enterprise. Franchisees must be clearly aware of how the franchisor obtains profit and that the franchisor is not taking two bites at the cherry by adding excessive mark-ups in addition to charging a management services fee or royalty. Transparency in dealings between franchisor and franchisee should be a cornerstone of the special franchisor-franchisee relationship.

Advertising levy. This is not an extra source of income for the franchisor. Franchisees may be required to pay an ongoing advertising levy to fund regional or national advertising and promotional campaigns. The levy is usually charged as a percentage of net sales, and should be separately accounted for by the franchisor. Often any overspend in one year is made up from the following year's account and any underspend is carried forward to the following year. The franchisee may also be required to allocate extra funds to promote his or her franchise locally.

Lease premium. When acquiring rented premises, a sum of money known as a lease premium is sometimes required by the landlord before the tenancy can be taken up. This payment is in addition to any prepayment of rent. It must be remembered that allowance for lease premium is never included in a franchisor's calculations of likely start-up costs.

Franchise renewal or sale

Another financial consideration arises if and when the franchise term is to be renewed. Does the franchisor have the right to make further charges at the time, or to increase the services fee? The franchise agreement needs close scrutiny on these points. It is normally agreed that no renewal fee will be charged. However, it is usual for the franchisor's legal costs renewing the franchise agreement to be paid by the franchisee, in the same way that a landlord usually expects a tenant to cover both parties' legal costs when a tenancy agreement is signed or renewed. A renewal charge may therefore be specified in the franchise agreement.

If you decide to sell your franchise, the franchisor will have some claim to a proportion of the sale price achieved. The actual figure will be calculated according to the formula set out in your franchise agreement. The amount will normally be increased if the franchisor finds a suitable buyer on your behalf and, as noted in Chapter 2, the proposed purchaser must be acceptable to the franchisor.

The franchise agreement must be closely examined at the outset to identify clearly all the financial implications of the contract.

Business funding

The two main financial needs of your business will be cash and capital, each carefully planned over the short, medium and long term to ensure survival, stability and growth. The advice of an experienced independent accountant before you start is invaluable – and will probably save considerable cost and anguish later on.

Cash. In the short term, and ongoing, your business must generate and retain cash. It is cash that pays the bills, enabling you to meet day-to-day commitments and stay in business. A common reason for the failure of businesses is that they simply run out of money. Many potentially profitable ventures collapse for the want of planning and control of 'cash flow' – that which flows out of the business must be replaced by fresh supplies flowing in!

Cash flows out in many ways: to pay suppliers, utilities, overheads, wages, advertising, management services fees or royalties, tax and VAT, as well as interest and capital repayments on loans and, not least, your own salary. Additionally, cash should be set aside over time for replacing worn out equipment, machinery or vehicles that have depreciated in resale value, as well as to meet the needs of refurbishing premises, fixtures and fittings. Against these outflows the only cash flowing into the business, other than by way of further capital injection, is that which comes from customers.

The business itself can have various 'sponges' that soak up valuable cash and prevent it being used for other purposes. One such sponge can be the stocking of products, another is credit purchases by customers.

Stock. Your business may necessitate stock-holding, which can be planned for as a 'working capital' cost. Any decision to buy more raw material or product stock other than that required to satisfy realistic customer expectations should be viewed as investment expenditure. In this case, the proposed benefit of such outlay can be assessed against the cost of funding it, and the increased risk of not achieving at least normal margin or return on investment.

Holding too much stock ties up working capital and may have practical implications for storage and handling, as well as increasing the risks of damage or obsolescence, and possibly raising insurance cover. The costs associated with these factors must be taken into account. On the other hand, holding too little stock may lead to lost orders, poor customer service or expensive panic buying.

Constant monitoring of sales trends and realistic forecasting help to identify optimum stock levels, achieving the most efficient balance for the amount of cash tied up before each sale is made.

Customer credit. In a retail operation, sales are usually for cash. If in your proposed business customers are normally invoiced instead of paying in cash, they are being given a measure of credit. Such customers are debtors and it is important to remember that debtors are using your money all the time that your invoice to them remains unpaid.

The amount of credit you allow to customers must be predetermined and clearly set out in your terms and conditions of sale. The total cash tied up as customer credit adds to the amount of working capital needed to run your business. Credit control is therefore vital to your business survival and is, in effect, the tap controlling the flow of available cash to your business arising from sales. The ways in which you enforce credit policies involve a balance between what is necessary to close each sale and the risk of incurring loss through late payment or bad debt.

For each sale it is wise to consider the ability of your business to withstand unpaid debt, or delayed payment. Your credit policies may need to be adjusted for customers in order to minimise the risk of loss. Distinctions can be made between regular customers, new or one-off buyers and the size of order involved. Obtaining a deposit and interim payments for large orders from new or existing customers can alleviate concerns over payment on both sides. You may also request, and follow up, references supplied by your prospective customer or, indeed, undertake a suitable credit check.

Providing a high-quality service or product will help the customer to value your business relationship and may make debt collection less difficult. Processing and delivering orders as quickly as possible, followed by accurate invoices submitted immediately after the sale has taken place, will reduce delay and possible excuses for non-payment by the customer.

The process of 'factoring' may be applicable to your business, as a way of reducing the amount of working capital you need. Factoring involves routinely transferring your invoices at a discount to a specialist factoring company, in return for your gaining immediate cash payment for the balance. Your customers are requested to pay their bills to the factoring company. Factoring money can be at least as expensive as a bank overdraft and is in practice usually 'with recourse'. This means that you have not sold your invoices outright. If the factoring company does not obtain the money from your customer, it will ask you for it.

Allowing credit to your customer naturally affects the relationship between you both. The word 'relationship' takes on an extended dimension and you may worry that your concerns over payment will lose you sales which are otherwise profitable. Good credit management is perhaps a matter of being as confident as possible that you have 'installed fences at the top of the cliff', rather than 'rushing ambulances to the bottom'.

Your franchisor should be able to advise you on established policies and procedures of customer credit and your expected management of it. Allowing customers to take unapproved credit from your business directly affects your planned cash position, shifting the working capital requirements from their business on to you and increasing yours. Credit policy and credit control, together with stockholding and stock control, should be viewed as integral parts of your total business funding programme.

Your creditors. Money you owe is a source of funds to your business: you have the use of your suppliers' money until you pay them.

Again, it is a matter of balance, since paying creditors too early increases the amount of cash required as working capital. However, discounts for early payment may be given, which offset the temporary use of extra cash. Persistent late payment on your part will sour your relationship with your supplier, and will inevitably damage your reputation. This may easily translate into financial penalties on further orders such as higher price quotations or the stipulation of more onerous terms for supply. In many franchises, the principal supplier is the franchisor with whom you have already negotiated terms.

Creditor control, then, is also a key to cash control. Astute awareness of your suppliers' own credit policies and controls can help to reduce the cash you need to have tied up in your own working capital.

Capital. This describes the total funds needed to set up and run your business, including cash. The cash required has been termed 'working capital'. The remaining capital is that to be spent on fixed assets: those items you need to buy, but not sell again, as part of your normal day-to-day business.

Capital expenditure can include such major items as property purchase or lease premium, refurbishment, fixtures and fittings, office and other equipment, machinery and vehicles to be used by the business. There will also be an initial fee to pay the franchisor at the outset.

As the business progresses over time, further capital expenditure will undoubtedly be required, if only to replace depreciated items where the replacement cost exceeds the amount of cash you may have retained for the purpose.

The franchisor under whose name you trade may impose strict regulations for maintaining image, quality or safety standards after your initial launch. These could mean undertaking substantial refurbishment or replacement at certain times and at considerable cost, throughout the life of your business. So, forecasting your capital requirements for as far ahead as you can see is a fundamental aspect of your financial plan.

It is also prudent to envisage at the outset the ultimate end of your business life. Many business guides and textbooks omit comment on this inevitable fate, but it is a subject well worth considering. It would be a foolish pilot who takes off on a flight, not having planned how, where and when the aircraft is to be landed!

The fact that your business flies the franchisor's colours means that you will not have total independence of decision when it comes to sale, or closure of the business. Your franchise agreement will probably not allow you to assign the business to anyone else. It will normally be time-bound so that, apart from outright sale to an approved third party, you are, effectively, locked in. Equally, at the end of the period of agreement, you could be locked out. In this respect a fixed-term agreement, without reasonable rights of renewal, could mean that your business as a whole becomes a depreciating asset.

Your franchisor is unlikely to terminate your involvement in the business if you are successful and not in breach of your franchise agreement. Your agreement may allow ongoing rights of renewal that are not to be unreasonably withheld by the franchisor – but this must be checked by your solicitor. What happens if the franchisor eventually decides that it wants to run its own company-owned and managed operation in your territory? Your franchisor's current management team may comprise entirely different people in the future, or indeed the whole company could be sold on to new owners with different ideas.

A range of future possibilities should be contemplated, including what would happen in the event of your own death or incapacity to manage the business. What happens if sickness or accident prevents you from fulfilling your side of the agreement? What are the financial implications of illness or accident if you are running a 'job' franchise of the kind described on page 27?

You will have to judge for yourself whether these scenarios are at all likely and just what they would mean in financial terms to you. Do you need to consider paying for specific insurance policies to minimise the financial risks?

It is perhaps obvious that the real value of your franchise lies in its ability to make and sustain all the profit you need within the term of the agreement, rather than capital gain from sale of the business. Your financial planning should reflect this strategy, and calculation of the 'pay-back period' for your investment becomes even more relevant perhaps than for a strategy which is not time-bound.

Pay-back period is the forecast length of time it will take for the business to generate sufficient income to return the amount of investment to which it relates. You may decide to include in this sum a calculation for the amount of interest that your capital might have earned if invested elsewhere, for example, in a building society or other savings account. The calculation of return on capital employed may be another useful indicator of the viability of the franchise and your accountant should be able to advise you on this.

Your enterprise may well require a varying blend of different types of finance when you launch and then as the size or nature of your business develops.

Sources of finance

The amount of your own investment must be considered first. Banks and other lenders like to know that the person to whom they are lending is deeply committed to the success of their enterprise; your own large monetary investment in your capabilities and your business plan is tangible proof of your commitment. Your money is at risk before everyone else's, as owners and shareholders are the last people to recoup money when a business collapses. You must be certain that you have considered all the likely dangers, and that the proposed returns will be greater than the interest you could receive by investing your cash elsewhere.

Franchisors will often have funding 'packages' already arranged in principle with perhaps a number of the larger banks. This does not mean that the bank recommends the franchise; it simply means that the bank has been approached by the franchisor to possibly provide funds to its franchisees.

The franchisor will have given the bank its accounts and model forecast projections for an average franchise operation. Normally the bank will have seen the franchise agreement and other supporting information relating to the franchise offer. Of course, the bank may also have first-hand knowledge of franchise performance from the accounts of existing franchisees who use its services.

Agreement for funding in principle is not a guarantee of any sort. However, it does tell you that a knowledgeable third party has had sight of all the relevant franchise documents and that the franchisor has been confident enough about the business offer to subject it to that process. Also, while the franchisor may be reluctant fully to expose to you all the accounts relating to its total business, it will have little choice but to do so to the bank if it wants to gain the bank's support.

To some extent money can be viewed as a commodity: there are money 'markets' and the cost of using money can fluctuate widely according to its source, when it is drawn upon, and by whom. Raising money to finance the purchase and launch of a franchise is treated in the same way as raising money to start any new business. However, most of the clearing banks do have specialist franchise units and/or the required expertise at commercial branch level and, generally, they

look more favourably on the average franchise application than on the average independent start-up. This is because a franchise is considered a lower risk to a lender for the reasons outlined above. Furthermore a bank will generally require that a prospective franchisee contributes a proportion of the start-up capital, around 30–50 per cent, from their personal resources. Any loan, plus interest, will need to be repaid before the end of the franchise term and the bank will look for collateral as security against default.

Taking out a loan can enable you to build the business without the pressures of short-term debt. It is important to match the features of the loan with the need for which it is required and the life of the project. Loans may be available for terms of more than three years, although normally they will not be for longer than the term of the franchise itself. The appropriate term, repayment schedule and interest rate should be chosen with care.

Banks are not necessarily your first port of call for business funding to add to your own equity but they are usually the obvious choice for most individuals starting up in business. The best advice is to shop around, preferably before visiting your own bank manager. Practice can improve your style and preparedness for answering questions. Presentation of your business plan is almost as important as its content, particularly if the document has to be forwarded for assessment to an office remote from the branch you visit.

The terms of borrowing will vary from bank to bank. The period of the loan can be negotiated to match your anticipated needs and the interest rate can be fixed, variable, or sometimes at a monthly managed rate. Loans require repayments of interest together with a portion of the capital on a regular basis. On larger loans it is sometimes possible to negotiate a repayment holiday on the capital element, whereby you pay only the interest for the first year or two.

Overdrafts are a common form of bank lending intended to meet relatively short-term finance needs. Many people start up in business with the help of an overdraft facility from their bank. That is, the actual amount on loan to them varies with their day-to-day needs, although it is limited to an agreed maximum ceiling. The interest rate, which may be negotiated, is usually linked to base rate and is therefore variable. The amount may be calculated on a daily balance or maximum demand basis within each period.

An arranged overdraft is comparatively less expensive than other types of short-term money and can be quickly set up. The arranged overdraft limit should not be exceeded without the bank manager's permission. An unarranged overdraft will quickly lead to bouncing cheques, cancelled payment mandates and punitive charges. While a loan would not be called in unless its payment terms were breached, the bank can demand instant repayment or reduction of an overdraft at any time. This could happen if you exceed the agreed overdraft ceiling without prior approval from the bank.

The type of funding 'package' you can get from the bank by way of overdraft, loan, or both, depends on your reasons for application, the viability of your business plan, your personal financial credibility, your own level of investment, and the amount you borrow compared with the amount of your own investment. It also depends on what security you can offer as collateral.

Security. Banks lend money that has been entrusted to them by others, so their first duty is to their depositors and shareholders. They will consider helping to finance a viable business plan, but they will not speculate. Consequently, banks will usually look for some form of security to safeguard the money that they allow you to put at risk. If you are keen to go ahead and have assets available this may seem no more than a formality. However, giving the bank a charge over your personal assets, or those of your company, requires very careful consideration. If the business fails it could result in the loss of all the assets you possess, including your home.

Even if you have formed a limited company, the bank manager is likely to require you to give a personal guarantee, in the absence of sufficient assets in the business. The security you may be asked for could be in the form of a floating charge over all your assets – a charge that could ultimately force you into personal bankruptcy. A charge placed against specific property is therefore normally to be preferred.

As a self-employed sole-trader or partner, you are personally liable for any debts incurred. As already noted, in a partnership, each partner is jointly and severally liable for all debts, irrespective of which partner incurred them. Having a written partnership agreement drawn up before you start trading is strongly recommended, even between husband and wife or other family members.

A written guarantee from a third party offered as security would usually be supported by a charge over property or other assets that they have. Another form of security could be a legal charge over any life policy you have with a surrender value. This would be assigned to the bank and, in the event of your death, the bank will automatically be repaid. Other financial assets such as a portfolio of shares in large, well-known companies can be pledged as security to the bank if their total value exceeds the amount borrowed by a large margin, to allow for fluctuating stock market values.

A limited company can use its property, assets, and even money owed to it, as security for a loan. This is known as a mortgage debenture and it must be registered at Companies House. The bank takes a floating charge over the assets, which means that the bank has first title to the company assets, but the company can use them without affecting the security.

The Loan Guarantee Scheme. In 1981 the Government set up the Loan Guarantee Scheme to help small entrepreneurs who had no security, such as a house, to offer and were therefore having difficulty borrowing money either to set up a new business or expand an existing one. In July 1993 a new version of the scheme was launched. Under the current scheme for new businesses the government guarantees 70 per cent of the loan up to £100,000 (85 per cent in Inner City Task Force and City Challenge areas). All loans are repayable over periods of two to seven years with up to a two-year capital repayment holiday.

A guarantee premium of 2.5 per cent is charged based on the amount of the loan (1 per cent in Inner City Task Force and City Challenge areas). An important change was the introduction of a fixed-rate loan alternative under the scheme, with typical rates being 10.75 per cent for loans up to £15,000 and 10.5 per cent for larger ones. Banks may still require a life insurance policy to be taken out by applicants to cover the amount of the loan.

However, as part of the changes, very small business and many of those operating in the retail sector were no longer eligible. Except for certain inner city areas, a lower limit of £5,000 was introduced. The scheme was also closed to certain new businesses setting up at the expense of an existing one in the same district. Those specifically excluded were most types of retailing, hairdressing, motor vehicle repair, and taxi and cab hire. The small business loan guarantee scheme may or may not be applicable to your personal circumstances and type of business proposed.

Application forms are available only from lenders involved in the scheme. In the first instance applicants should contact the lender with a view to obtaining a conventional loan or overdraft. Only if conventional lending is denied, through a lack of security or track record, can the loan guarantee scheme be considered. For further details of the scheme, the useful *Loan Guarantee Scheme* booklet is available from the Department of Trade and Industry (DTI).

Of course, when a business depends too much on borrowed money, interest payments could cripple it. Ideally, net trading profits before interest and taxation should be at least twice the total of the interest payments.

Equity. Your financial stake in your business is termed equity and represents your ownership of the enterprise. You may choose, or need, to share ownership with other stakeholders who also contribute equity capital to the business in return for shares or a partnership arrangement. Immediate thoughts turn to relatives, friends, former work colleagues and other close contacts who may be interested in helping to support the business financially. When raising capital from these sources, you must yourself be satisfied that you will be able to get along together and that you have common short-term and long-term objectives.

You may consider sharing the business ownership with someone who has skills and experience that complement your own. This could enable the business to be built on the combination of your joint strengths and minimise the effects of possible areas of individual lack of expertise. You would also feel happier about following advice from someone who has a financial interest in the company's survival and overall prosperity.

The Enterprise Investment Scheme. If you are to operate as a limited company and you believe that you will be able to attract outside equity finance, the government has introduced the Enterprise Investment Scheme (EIS), which allows tax benefits to people investing in British business. Details are available from your local tax office and the DTI publish a useful booklet. Your accountant should also be a reliable source of advice on your overall personal plans as well as those for your business.

Launched on 1 January 1994, the Enterprise Investment Scheme replaced the former Business Expansion Scheme (BES), operating since 1981, which was failing to attract private investment into small unquoted companies outside the property sector. The EIS provides a range of tax incentives to encourage individuals to invest in new, full-risk ordinary shares of certain types of high-risk unquoted trading companies. Investors can claim up-front income tax relief at the lower rate of tax, currently 20 per cent on up to £100,000 of qualifying investment in any tax year from 1994–1995 onwards. They must hold the shares for at least five years in order to keep that income tax relief, but having done so, any profits arising from disposal of the shares an exempt from capital gains tax. Also, any losses arising on disposal of the shares may be set against chargeable income or capital gains tax, provided claim is made within prescribed time limits.

To qualify for the tax relief the investor must not be connected with the company. Special rules allow investors who wish to be involved with the management of the company to become 'Business Angels' by taking up paid directorships once they have purchased some EIS shares.

Companies qualifying for the scheme will be able to raise up to £1m a year through the issue of EIS shares. Most trading companies will qualify for the scheme, although there are certain excluded activities that are likely to debar franchisors. There are a number of other conditions that need to be satisfied by both the company and the investor(s).

The EIS may therefore be attractive to franchisees who set up limited companies and who wish to raise additional, outside finance by issuing equity. They may choose to use the scheme at the outset or once the business has been running for some time and is ready to expand. Further information can be found in the booklet *A Guide to the Enterprise Investment Scheme*, available from the DTI.

Leasing. Leasing may be worth considering as a means of obtaining some of your fixed assets. Although you will never own the equipment, the main advantage is that significant capital outlay is avoided, which can be a big help to cash flow. All payments made under the lease are treated as expenses on which you can claim full tax relief.

There are different sorts of lease. An *open-ended lease* allows you to end it whenever you like after the expiry of an agreed minimum period. A *closed-ended lease* is usually for a fixed term of one to five years, after which there may be an option to take on a further lease for a nominal rent, or you may have an option to buy the item. A *balloon lease* lets you make part of the capital payment at the end of the lease, effectively reducing the monthly lease payments beforehand.

Contract hire. This is a form of leasing, usually negotiated to finance a fleet of vehicles or quantities of goods used in the operation of a business, for example table linen or china for caterers. Individual items are not specified; the hire covers an agreed number of an overall specification for a given period of time, usually with other relevant clauses included in the contract.

Hire purchase. At the end of a prescribed hire period, you gain outright ownership of the asset. This has the advantage that capital outlay is avoided, helping cash flow. However, the amount of interest payable may be at a significantly greater rate than an equivalent bank loan. Your accountant will be able to advise you on the tax relief arrangements for capital allowances and interest payments.

Grants and other forms of assistance

You may be able to attract grant funding, preferential loans, or allowances aimed at helping small business development. These are available from a variety of sources, including central government initiatives, local authorities wishing to encourage local enterprise and some charities specifically targeting certain groups of people or types of local industry.

A focal point for much of the government's assistance is your regional Training and Enterprise Council (TEC) in England and Wales, or the Local Enterprise Companies (LECs) in Scotland.

These offer: business information, advice and counselling; financial help to assist unemployed people start up new businesses; a variety of courses in business skills; help with the costs of consultancy to develop staff and meet future skills needs; and help for firms wishing to train young people or adults. The Scottish LECs also cover assistance to businesses previously offered by the Scottish Development Agency and the Highlands and Islands Development Board.

The Business Start-Up Scheme (BSUS) was introduced in 1991 and has provided direct financial assistance with appropriate business training and advice to unemployed people who wish to start up in business. The scheme does not exclude franchises, but each regional TEC and LEC has its own arrangements regarding the terms of the financial support and business coaching that it offers to suitable candidates. You are advised to contact your regional TEC or LEC direct.

If your franchise is in a different region from your home, it is worth approaching the TEC or LEC in both regions to find the best help available for your circumstances. Attitudes about supporting prospective franchisees do vary from region to region, even though the average properly structured and ethically managed franchise has a statistically far better chance of survival than the average new independent business. On request, regional offices will send you their free information packs describing what they have to offer, and they generally have facilities for discussing your particular needs in person.

Assistance for start ups is available from a UK network of over 400 independent, privately run Local Enterprise Agencies and, in Scotland, Enterprise Trusts. All offer business advice, counselling and, in many cases, additional services such as access to loan funds, managed workspaces, business clubs and information services. Your regional TEC or LEC will be able to advise you which Enterprise Agency covers your area. In Northern Ireland the local Enterprise Development Unit (LEDU) provides comprehensive information and advisory services and financial help to small firms employing up to 50 people.

The Business Links network has created some 200 'one stop shops' for business support throughout the UK. Each Business Link is open to all businesses, including franchisees, free of charge. They offer advice, information and access to specialists. Information available may include details of schemes providing financial assistance to new businesses.

Scottish Business Shops are based at 41 locations throughout Scotland and maintain two databases of interest to potential franchisees. The FAST database provides information on all the grants and loans that are available from Local Enterprise Councils, local authorities and government and non-government sources. The FRANCIS database contains valuable information on over 300 franchisors in Scotland. It lists the benefits and drawbacks, steps to becoming a franchisee, how to identify and assess an opportunity and how to finance a deal. A specialist business franchise counsellor is available for consultation and enquirers are welcome to return for as many counselling sessions as the counsellor feels are required. The above services are all offered free of charge. (For contact details of the Scottish Business Shops headquarters, see Chapter 10.)

Further government help may be available through the Loan Guarantee Scheme (page 50), and special help may be available in inner cities as part of the government's Action for Cities programme. Inner City Task Forces, which operate within 16 urban areas, help small businesses with grants and loans through their Task Force Development Funds. City Action Teams coordinate government programmes in the inner cities and can offer extra support to individual projects that are not eligible for main programme funding.

Help to small firms in certain urban areas is available from Urban Development Corporations and through the government's Urban Programme, which is run through local authorities. The programme can provide help with renting premises and with training for suitable applicants.

You will find your local Department of Trade and Industry (DTI) office very helpful on a whole range of business issues and early contact is recommended. The regional office of the DTI will be listed in your local telephone directory.

If your business is to be located out of town, the Rural Development Commission (RDC) may be of assistance. The RDC has been helping to develop rural businesses for a number of years and will send you a useful free information pack about its programmes on request. The RDC provides businesses in rural England with free general advice and in-depth technical and professional support including skills training, for which a charge is usually made. The Commission also provides help in converting and acquiring business premises (including financial assistance in designated development areas), limited loan facilities and grants for exhibition participation and marketing consultancy.

The objective of the RDC loan fund is to provide topping-up finance to small firms within the designated priority areas of rural England, to maintain existing employment and to help create new job opportunities. Loans are available for buildings, equipment and working capital, with a minimum of £5,000. The normal maximum is £75,000 but applications for higher amounts may be considered. In general, loans are limited to 50 per cent of project costs, although in exceptional cases this may be raised to 70 per cent. Working capital loans however, cannot be greater than the applicant's own financial investment in the business.

The RDC also provides discretionary grants for the refurbishment of redundant buildings in priority areas, to bring them back into productive business use or to enhance their current use. The objectives are both to utilise existing assets to the full and to provide new employment opportunities. Enquiries should be directed to your nearest RDC office.

In addition to the service arranged by Welsh TECs, help for business in Wales is available from the Welsh Development Agency, and in mid-Wales, from the Development Board for Rural Wales. These services include industrial property to rent or buy, loan and equity finance and special help from high-tech industry inward investment businesses.

Local authorities often provide help with business start-up. Their assistance may be in the form of grants and/or loans, business advice and premises. Again, your local telephone directory is a good starting point for contacting county, borough and district councils.

In former coal-mining areas, there may be regional help with loans, advice and premises. The interest is economic regeneration of the local area, so you do not have to be a former British Coal employee to qualify for assistance. Similarly, British Steel Industry Ltd helps businesses to start up, expand or relocate in traditional steel areas.

Grants and cheap loans are available from the Prince's Youth Business Trust for young people starting up in self-employment. To qualify you need to be aged between 18 and 25, or 30 in the case of disabled persons. Its grants are designed to cover specific items and loans and are available towards the cost of capital equipment or to help fund working capital. A loan is usually free of interest for the first year, with a repayment holiday for the first six months. A low rate of interest is charged in years two and three.

The Prince's Scottish Youth Business Trust operates in Scotland.

5

Your own closer look

You may have started to think about taking up a franchise for a host of different reasons; people are drawn to the idea by many routes. For some it is one particular business or type of business that attracts attention, for others the appeal is of franchising as a concept and they have no particular type of business in mind.

People who do investigate the idea a little further are often amazed to discover such a wide diversity of choice on offer. It is not surprising that many find the scene unfamiliar and confusing. A structured analysis of the options might be useful at this point, either to fully evaluate an already favoured franchise against its 'competitors' in the same market, or to rationally review as many of the options as possible.

There are three fundamental areas to consider when surveying the range of franchises available. As most people already have a great many demands placed on their time and energy, making a choice within each area should enable you to narrow the field to manageable proportions. This in turn should allow you to investigate more fully the individual opportunities that broadly fit your requirements.

The first priority must be to determine your level of capital investment. A good starting point would be to calculate your 'net worth'. That is, to add up the amount of any debts and loans to which you are committed, such as mortgages, bank borrowings, outstanding credit card balances, hire purchase balances remaining, etc. Then deduct the total figure from the actual value of all your realisable assets which may include cash, savings, property, shares and surrender values on life assurance policies. It is then a matter of deciding what proportion of your net worth you are prepared to risk as your personal investment of capital. Any business borrowing requirement should be strictly assessed against the realistic cash flow and profitability forecasts contained in the business plan for your proposed franchise operation.

Having decided on your own financial terms of reference, the other two main features to consider are the type of distribution envisaged, and whether you would prefer a franchise that predominantly serves other businesses, or one that deals mostly with the public.

The range and scope of opportunities are often categorised by market sector (the product or service provided) discussed in Chapter 2, but ideally you will need to carry out some desk research at this point to identify franchises that fit the type of business you are seeking. This may be van based, mobile, depot based, retail outlet, or one which you can run from home; it may be business to business, or providing products or services to the general public. Deciding the actual product or service to provide can come later in this decision-making process, unless, of course, you have a strong interest or background in a particular market that you are keen to pursue.

Your research should cover the various franchise publications, directories and handbooks, visits to franchise exhibitions and requests for brochures from likely franchisors. None of these activities places you under any obligation whatsoever. They do, however, allow you either to confirm your original decisions or re-examine exactly what it is you are looking for. Once you have a broad picture in your mind of the type of business you anticipate, you will be able to consider more clearly the various products or services that are sold within that framework.

Having worked through a structured survey of the options, you will be ready to examine specific franchise opportunities in detail. You will have gained a first impression of the 'style' of each franchisor in your selected type of business. How you were treated on the telephone when you requested a brochure, whether your request was dealt with efficiently and courteously, and the standard of material provided to you, will give you clues as to how the various franchisors might approach further business dealings with you.

As already mentioned, successful franchising is dependent on the quality of the franchisor/franchisee relationship. In this respect, the 'chemistry' must be right from the start. Your eventual franchisor should obviously be someone you can trust. You should feel comfortable talking to each member of the franchisor's management team. The overall business manner of the franchisor, the ethos of the company, and the product or service itself should give you a 'buzz'. This may not be an aspect of your decision-making until perhaps several meetings have taken place between yourself and the franchisor and your professional advisers have had sight of the franchise agreement, cash flow and profitability forecasts. However, everything about the style of the franchise should appeal to you, and match your most positive expectations.

Before looking at the actual business offer contained in the franchise agreement and detailed model forecasts provided by the franchisor, it is worth taking time to research for yourself the following:

- the background and established track record of the franchisor;
- the market in which the business operates, both nationally and within the area of your choice;
- the viability of the proposed product or service in that market;
- the viability of the chosen route to the market;
- the product or service itself;
- the real value of the trading name in the market;
- the financial, organisational, security and safety controls needed;
- the availability of funding, in principle.

The franchisor

Undertake your own thorough research into the company: its background; true size and financial standing; its reputation in the market; and, where possible, its reputation among other franchisees in its network. The business section of your local country library will be an excellent place to start. Ask for any published financial information about the company and its own parent company if applicable. For the most recent figures, you may decide to carry out a company search and the library may have on-line facilities for this. If it does not, contact Companies House yourself by telephone for advice on procedure. Fees will be charged according to the depth of information sought.

You may already have an idea of the company's reputation, but talking to as many people as possible can only be helpful in gaining a better view.

Is the company a member of the British Franchise Association (BFA)? Belonging to the BFA is certainly not compulsory and many reputable firms have not sought membership. However, members will have undergone a vetting procedure and will have agreed to abide by the BFA's published code of ethics.

Who are the franchisor's principal officers? What are their backgrounds and experience? Have they been involved in previous business failures, or ever been made personally bankrupt? County court judgments are a matter of public record and there are credit reference firms in the *Yellow Pages* who will check such information for you, for a suitable fee.

Who are the true owners of the business, that is the major shareholders? Again, seek advice from your local business library, or carry out a company search.

How long has the company been trading? At what stage did it start franchising? Why did it choose the franchise route for expansion? How many franchisees are there in the network? How many have there been? Have any failed? How many more franchisees are yet to be recruited? For answers to these questions you may have to wait until you are in closer discussion with the franchisor and until you can identify and talk to one of the early franchisees.

How does the company make its profit? Is its profit made through management services fees/royalties or through a mark-up on products supplied to franchisees? How 'transparent' are its dealings with franchisees?

What initial and ongoing backing or support will you be given as a franchisee? Details of what you can legally expect will be contained in the franchise agreement, but this should not preclude initial enquiries. For example, how many field service staff does the company employ in relation to the size of its network?

What initial and ongoing training can you expect and who pays the costs? Again, details will be in the franchise agreement but you may be able to find out at an early stage of your enquiries how many trainers the company employs, where the initial training takes place and how long it lasts.

How sophisticated is the franchisor's communications system? Does the franchisor respond efficiently to requests for advice or support? What communications will you receive on financial information, market intelligence, performance data? The specifics of this may not appear in the franchise agreement, but you may be able to obtain from existing franchisees a broad idea of the level of feedback and quality of communications normally provided.

Will you receive help to draw up your business plan? You should be responsible for constructing your own business plan, but realistic sales forecasts and some market research data should be forthcoming from the company, using proven results gained elsewhere and clearly showing any assumptions that have been made. An 'off the shelf' business plan from the franchisor should not be acceptable. Figures that are an amalgam of those proved elsewhere will not necessarily relate exactly to your own proposed territory, and indeed may reflect trading results of a more prosperous economic climate. The franchise brochure may outline what help you can expect to receive. (Business planning is addressed fully in Chapter 7.)

The market

A good business idea and a good trade name are two essentials for business success, but the fact remains that without customers you do not have a business at all. The market should be clearly identifiable and quantified. You should know what sort of customers you will be looking for, where they are and how to reach them within your proposed territory.

You need to know how their needs are currently being satisfied, and whether there is a genuine gap in the market that your proposed franchise can exploit. If there appears to be an opportunity, research further, until you are certain that there is a market within your proposed territory.

Even general polite enquiries to other operators, relevant trade associations and the editors of trade journals can be enlightening, particularly during the early stages of your research. Of course, you will have to decide how much of your own plans you are willing to divulge to each person.

Meaningful research should identify the relevant current size and potential for growth of the market as a whole and for your proposed territory in particular. This also means that the market 'width' and 'depth' should be identified, defining the types and numbers of prospective customers, where they can be found and how their needs for the product or service are currently satisfied. How is the size of a territory determined? What sort of territory might you be offered and how does it vary from that used in the pilot operation(s) or other sources of model figures for financial forecasting? Has the business really been proven, tried and tested? At what stage is the overall market in terms of its life-cycle: is it expanding, relatively stable, or declining?

Research should also reveal the observable trends and those that can reasonably be predicted when all factors influencing the market are taken into account. Such factors may include the uses of the product or service, as well as the social, political, economic and technological changes that can be reasonably foreseen. Similarly, what are the future activities of competitors likely to be? That is, what opportunities and threats are facing the business?

You will need to be aware of the exact nature of the market you will be in. Who and what competes for the customers' money that you want to be spent on your products or service? Is your market (and profit) to be found in just selling products or will you be providing a service, the quality of which enables you to charge a premium? For example, if you are to run a pub franchise, your customers will almost certainly consider that you are providing a hospitality/leisure service and not just selling a range of drinks and snacks. Selling luxury fountain pens may face less competition from ball-points and fibre-tips than other products in the adult gift market, such as cigarette lighters, silk scarves and cuff-links. Here, packaging, presentation and perceived value are more important than price alone. This is also an example of where the value of a respected brand name scores heavily.

The route to the market

How do competitors supply their market? Does the franchise follow this route, or does it use a different means? Can it afford to be different? Does the way the franchise approaches the market offer benefits to the customer for which extra margin or competitive advantage is obtained? Is any such competitive advantage sustainable in the longer term?

Territorial considerations may need to be taken into account. Where do other franchisees of the same business impinge on your scope of activity? Where might you impinge on theirs? What are the tangible marketing benefits of being in the 'network'?

The product or service

Be wary of revolutionary new or relatively unproven products and concepts. Remember that most franchise agreements will tie you to the product or service for a minimum of perhaps five years or more. Viable customer demand must be capable of outliving the franchise term! It is surprisingly easy to be carried away by the novelty factor of the latest fad or fashion. Sales figures quoted to you by an exuberant franchisor may well have been achieved in the first flush of launch into the market, before competitors have crowded in.

The product or service must offer a 'unique selling proposition' (USP). That is, a valid reason for customers to buy from you rather than from other companies in the same market. The USP is what gives you a competitive edge. It may not rest solely with the product or service but may be derived from other factors, such as speed of service and flexibility of delivery. The secret recipe of Colonel Sanders' Kentucky Fried Chicken is a good example of a USP, backed up by the style and method of its retailing. Without a sustainable USP, the business idea might be easily and successfully copied by others (or yourself!).

The margin you can obtain must allow for your viable business survival, development and growth. An old adage says that profit is made when you buy and realised when you sell. Even providing a service that has no product sale attached to it requires close scrutiny of your true costs, expenses and commitment of time, in order to assess the final value to you of each sale. Your product or service should therefore be capable of maintaining its margin in the face of strong opposition based upon price alone.

The product or service should be safe and ethical, with no harmful effects for the environment.

The trading name

Is the trading name already well established? Does it have a good reputation? If relatively new, is the name memorable? Is it catchy and easily identified with the type of business being promoted? Will the name last the life of the business and allow for strategic market development if necessary?

Is there a logo that helps to identify the brand of product or service? A logo is a visual device or design that is specific to its owner. Franchise agreements refer to logos as 'proprietory marks', which remain the property of the franchisor, but which the franchisee is allowed to use. A highly distinctive logo and trading name can be of immense help in attracting customers within a strongly competitive marketplace such as in *Yellow Pages*' advertisements or in a crowded shopping centre.

It is important that the right to use the trading name and/or logo is clearly established – that the franchisor has title to it and the right to assign it for your use. It is worthwhile checking the Trade Marks Registry to ensure the logo or name has been registered by the company. Many businesses do not have a registered trade mark, which means you could have less protection than you are led to believe.

Financial, organisational, security and safety controls

What management information and financial control systems will you be expected to operate? These should be as straightforward as possible and directly relevant to your own needs. Accurate and timely administration of the business will be essential, but beware of becoming an unpaid administrator or analyst for the company's sole benefit. You may not gain a full view of what is involved until you undergo training in the business, but existing franchisees will be able to tell you how much time they spend each week on administrative duties.

The systems used in the administration of the franchise should generate full range of ongoing information that you are trained to interpret and understand. It will be necessary for you to adhere to such systems if you are to satisfy the franchisor's requirements for specific regular information and maintain control over your business. The most common cause of business failure among independent start-ups is their inability to keep proper accounting records. That franchisors invariably insist on using a proven system of accounting could well be one of the factors that make the average franchise more likely to succeed than the average independent business start-up.

The franchise should allow for time to review progress regularly, understand what the figures mean and respond effectively to them. Comparing results and performance with other franchisees in the network can help to identify areas that vary from the norm. Many franchise networks have their own franchise association to which all franchisees automatically belong, meeting regularly at regional and national levels. Where such associations do not exist formally, franchisees tend to get together to talk shop and gain mutual support and benefit from each other.

Constructing a detailed and comprehensive business plan before you start greatly reduces the risk of failure. Monitoring performance against the business plan, responding to variances to secure the progress of the plan, or indeed amending the plan in order to achieve your business and personal objectives, should become part of your daily business life.

You will need to be pro-active, driving the business forward, rather than responding reactively to unforeseen events. It will be your responsibility to control the pace and direction of the business in line with your obligations under the franchise agreement.

You will also be responsible for all aspects of security and safety, so it is worth considering the requirements in these areas at an early stage of your research. Substantial recent legislation has addressed a great many safety issues, particularly for businesses that employ staff. You will need to understand the implications of such legislation on the franchise and the cost of implementation. It is advisable to seek professional advice on this subject, but an invaluable source of reference, written in layman's terms, is *Croner's Reference Book for the Self-Employed and Smaller Business*.

Funding

The subject of funding in general is covered in Chapter 4; you will need to apply the relevant aspects to the specific franchise under consideration. Skilful planning and control of all funds to be used in the business is absolutely essential.

Forward planning is necessary to ensure that selected types of funding are used most cost-effectively – the right amounts from the right sources, at the right time and at the right price. Even if a franchisor has a funding package agreed in principle with a particular bank, it is well worth shopping around to obtain the optimum package to suit your particular needs.

In any new business start-up the margin for error is slim. You are strongly advised to consult an accountant who is experienced in the field you wish to enter. He or she should be able to offer advice on alternative sources of funding, grants and business start-up loans, as well as on your overall plans and personal tax position.

SWOT analysis

As a way of interpreting the results of your research on each possible franchise opportunity, it is a good idea to separate them into four categories: strengths, weaknesses, opportunities, and threats (SWOT). The strengths and weaknesses will generally be factors inherent in the business itself, while the opportunities and threats will be controlled by the external environment.

The SWOT analysis for your chosen venture should be included in the final business plan. It is also invaluable as a way of looking at the relative merits and pitfalls of each proposed venture and thereby assessing and directly comparing the risks in each.

You may find that a particular aspect is both a strength and, in a different way, a weakness. In this case it should appear in both sections. Strengths should be built on and developed; weaknesses recognised and minimised or circumvented. Likewise, opportunities may merely represent 'jam tomorrow' unless planned for, and threats (from competitor action, social or legal changes, or technological advances) may become very real, unless anticipated and dealt with as part of your ongoing business plan.

Advancing cautiously

When you have researched as much as you can from a distance, you are ready to decide whether to go to the next stage and formally approach the franchisor of your choice. Meeting with the franchisor is covered in Chapter 6.

It is worth remembering that you are under no obligation whatsoever until you actually sign the franchise agreement or preliminary purchase agreement. After meeting the franchisor, continue to seek further advice. Read any information you can obtain on franchising. Try to keep up to date with events and trends in the market you are considering. Maintain an awareness of exactly how much you can personally afford to invest or have tied up in the business.

Make your own choice of advisers, don't limit yourself to those suggested by the franchisor. Four very important people at this stage will be your bank manager, an independent accountant, a solicitor (preferably one with experience of franchising), and, if applicable, your partner or spouse. It also pays to talk to someone else you know who has been or is self-employed already, who can help you to assess the whole picture. Do retain a healthy measure of scepticism about franchises and franchisors; be sure that your own research and professional advice have covered all aspects before you sign any contract or agreement.

Running a franchise will involve a great deal of hard work and sustained effort. However, it can also yield substantial rewards, enjoyment and the sense of achievement that comes from running your own business and working for yourself.

6

Recruitment and selection

Franchisees come from many diverse backgrounds. Some take up a franchise following redundancy or early retirement from an employer, or completion of a fixed-term contract elsewhere. Others leave employment to fulfil their ambition of running their own business. Quite a few are already selfemployed and seek the business umbrella that franchising can offer.

You will find that all reputable franchisors operate their own recruitment and selection programmes. The idea of the franchise broker is very much frowned on within the industry as an agent selling franchises on a commission basis has no reason to be concerned about the franchisee's future. You are therefore advised to deal directly with the franchisor.

Franchisors attract prospective franchisees in a number of different ways. The best-known companies receive a great many speculative approaches and applications from individuals, some of whom have only that one company in mind. Generally, however, the onus is on the franchisor to attract the type of applicant they believe will be most successful in their network.

The recruitment methods used by franchisors include straightforward newspaper and magazine advertising. There are several magazines dedicated to franchising and many general business publications that carry articles about franchising and franchise recruitment advertisements. A number of the leading daily newspapers do likewise, and *The Express* has a regular feature each Monday.

Exhibitions provide excellent opportunities for the prospective franchisee to view the variety on offer and to meet and talk informally to those franchisors who are represented. Franchisors make use of exhibitions to distribute promotional literature and brochures, meet prospective applicants and arrange further meetings with interested enquirers. No reputable franchisor would expect to sign up franchisees on the spot. You would be wise to avoid any franchisor wanting you to do so on your first meeting, before you have been able to evaluate fully the franchise and take legal advice.

Permanent privately run exhibitions of promotional information from subscribing franchisors have been set up by the Franchise (Information) Centre in Manchester and London. Along with display advertising and information on companies that pay to be represented, the service also offers free independent advice on franchising as a whole.

All franchisors produce some form of brochure or information pack to give or send to enquirers, free of charge and with no obligation on either side. The standard of information and quality of presentation supplied varies enormously and there is no set format. However, most will include an application form, which may have to be completed before discussions are taken further.

When considering taking up a franchise, perhaps the most difficult assessment you are required to make is an assessment of yourself. You may find it useful to canvass the views of people close to you, who you feel can be objective. Any such assessment needs to cover four main issues: your motivation, your financial resources, your interests, and your personal characteristics. Use the self-assessment test below to help you towards an objective view of your personal characteristics.

It has been suggested that franchisees should possess the following characteristics:

- Willingness to work hard
- Desire to succeed
- Management ability
- Financial backing
- Strong 'people' skills
- Support from family.

You

Before applying for a franchise, putting yourself up for selection by your favoured franchisor, and perhaps embarking on a path that is not the right one for you, carry out a self-examination. This may also help to prepare you for the franchisor's assessment procedures. Your personal assessment needs to cover the following aspects of yourself:

- Your willingness to work hard.
- Your desire to succeed.
- Your ability to plan, implement and control the business in terms of your resources of time and money.
- Your likely attention to the administration and recording of financial information and your skill in managing finances.
- Your own personal objectives and clarity of purpose.
- Your temperament, attributes and abilities.
- Your capacity to learn and adapt.
- Your ability to capitalise on your strengths and to minimise the effect of your weaknesses.

Personal characteristics and capacities are often determinants of success in a business venture, which requires a fairly obsessive temperament and a capacity for dealing with stress.

Many people in business claim that their prime motivation is not money. In fact, many might earn more elsewhere, especially considering the effort and risks involved. They are concerned more with the nature of the activity, the emotional sense of involvement and personal satisfaction.

Being self-employed is a way of life, not just a job. Understanding yourself, your motivations, strengths and limitations will be a crucial ingredient for both initial and sustained success. Working successfully alongside an established company and its management will require a positive approach to the relationship by both parties.

Everyone has different personal strengths and limitations. Ask someone who knows you well to objectively assess your personal characteristics, using the following score sheet. Request that they cross a relevant dot alongside each characteristic, scoring you 9 for an obvious strength and 1 as the lowest score along the line. Then score each aspect for yourself, as objectively as possible, by putting a circle around a relevant dot on each line.

Where your circles do not match their crosses, check with the other person their reasons for scoring you as they have. Also, reconsider your own estimates in the light of the other person's opinion.

Personal Characteristics Score Sheet

Score 9 for any characteristic of obvious strength, score 1 as the lowest score. Mark only one position along each line.

Characteristic	**1**	**2**	**3**	**4**	**5**	**6**	**7**	**8**	**9**
Ability to work hard	.	.	.	.	.	.	.	.	.
Desire to succeed	.	.	.	.	.	.	.	.	.
Management ability	.	.	.	.	.	.	.	.	.
Financial awareness	.	.	.	.	.	.	.	.	.
'People' skills	.	.	.	.	.	.	.	.	.
Determination	.	.	.	.	.	.	.	.	.
Energy level	.	.	.	.	.	.	.	.	.
Ability to cope with stress	.	.	.	.	.	.	.	.	.
Independence	.	.	.	.	.	.	.	.	.
Ability to listen to others	.	.	.	.	.	.	.	.	.
Level of self-esteem	.	.	.	.	.	.	.	.	.
Ability to analyse risks	.	.	.	.	.	.	.	.	.
Ability to manage own time	.	.	.	.	.	.	.	.	.
Creativity/initiative	.	.	.	.	.	.	.	.	.

Use the results of this simple checklist to thoroughly examine your motives for self-employment. Plan ways in which you can build on your strengths and, importantly, how you will minimise the effects of your own limitations upon your business.

Making money work for you

There are two ways in which you can increase your prosperity: using your own labour, or using money to work for you. Your business will grow more swiftly and be more likely to succeed if you develop a clear understanding of how to make money work for you. Points covered in previous chapters are:

- Skilful planning and control of cash flow is absolutely essential.
- Knowledge and use of the most suitable types of funding available can make all the difference.
- Forward planning of all financial requirements to ensure funding is used most cost-effectively is necessary.
- In any new business start-up the margin for error is slim – consult an accountant who is experienced in the field you wish to enter.
- Pay attention to strengths, weaknesses, opportunities and threats (SWOT).

Support

You will need to be self-sufficient and resourceful enough to keep driving the business, but you must also be able to rely on the support of those around you, essentially your family. You should also be willing to seek out and use any external agencies that offer knowledgeable support and/or advice.

The franchisor should be willing and able to assist you in a number of ways and these could add real strength to your plans.

Meeting the franchisor

You may well be invited to visit a franchisor's head office for further discussion – and to be assessed as a potential franchisee. It is also your chance to assess them and to ask many questions. Chapter 5 contains details of the research that ideally you will have conducted prior to your first formal meeting with the franchisor.

Many of your questions will have been answered as you proceeded with your research before, during, and after your first formal meeting. However, you should be satisfied that the franchisor has covered all your points, or noticed if they were reluctant to give information without prompting from you.

At an early stage in your discussions with the franchisor you will be asked to complete an application form. This will not only cover basic information and your career history to date, but also a detailed examination of your financial situation. The franchisor will need to be sure that you would be able to proceed should you be selected. The application form should contain a statement that the information you have provided will remain confidential and will form the basis of any negotiations between you and the franchisor. It should of course be completed honestly and truthfully. The form should also make quite clear to you that completing it places you under no obligation whatsoever to proceed.

A confidentiality agreement may be included in the application form, but more usually it is a separate document for you to sign. The franchisor is in the difficult position of wanting to gain your further interest in the franchise offer without giving away too many secrets of the business. You should not sign any other document at your first meeting – nor should you be asked to. You should receive the clear impression that the franchisor is not so much trying to sell you a franchise as to helping you buy a business that is right for you.

During your first formal discussions with the franchisor, you should gain answers to any questions left unresolved from your initial research (see Chapter 5). It is a good idea to ask for the name of the firm of solicitors responsible for drawing up the franchise agreement. You can then check whether that firm is an affiliate of the BFA – if so, it will be reassuring to know that they not only have their own professional standards to abide by, but also those of the BFA.

You should be able to assess the franchisor's sincerity and commitment to franchising as a way of doing business. It is useful to find out the origins of the franchise strategy. Was the company specifically set up with franchising in mind, or did its franchising evolve as a natural response to marketing, rather than financial, needs? It is not unknown for a company to try to franchise its way out of financial difficulty, using the franchisee's investment of resources to make up for losses of its own. The franchisor should be very positive about developing ongoing relationships with its franchisees.

You will want to know the backgrounds of each of the principal officers of the business and with what other businesses they have been associated. You should ask whether any franchisees have failed and, if so, what causes were attributed to their failure. You should gain a clear overview of the market, and how the franchisor sees future trends developing for franchisees.

Some franchisors may ask you to complete a psychometric assessment. Such assessment procedures are now quite common among employers in the process of interviewing and selection. There are no right or wrong results; the analyses are carried out only to help identify certain personal characteristics and to match them against those that are considered desirable in a franchisee. The type of characteristics sought are described earlier in this chapter. The franchisor will be looking for you to exhibit those desirable personal qualities, as well as your financial ability to proceed. The franchisor, like you, will be assessing whether the 'chemistry' is right.

Your visit to the franchisor's premises should provide you with sufficient insight into the business for you to decide whether you wish to proceed to the next step. You should ask the franchisor for a complete list of all current franchisees. You will want to be able to choose for yourself those you would like to contact for their views on the franchise offer. Since existing franchisees will be bound by the confidentiality clause of their own franchise agreements, they will require reassurance from the franchisor that you are a genuine applicant with whom they can discuss their experience of the business.

Your next task is to visit and telephone as many of the existing franchisees as you need to satisfy your research. You will want to know what training, advice and support each has received and whether their original financial forecasts from the franchisor were achieved in practice. You should be able to picture yourself in their position, carrying on the business in similar fashion. You should gain insight into the existing franchisee/franchisor relationships, whether the balance of the 'partnership' is about right, or whether the franchisor is considered too intrusive or too remote. Remember that the franchisor may well ask those franchisees their opinions of you as a prospective 'partner' in the network.

Arrangements with the franchisor should have been left on the understanding that you will re-approach the company if you wish to proceed after your discussions with franchisees. In other words, that you decide whether you wish to proceed, again with no obligation, to the next step. The franchisor will also need to decide whether negotiations should continue.

For your second meeting, the franchisor may suggest visiting you at your home to discuss in detail the elements of the franchise agreement. A reputable franchisor will probably wish to meet your spouse or partner if you have one. Support from those close to you is vital for your success in business. The franchisor will want to avoid claims that you were rushed into a hasty agreement without due consultation with others close to you whose lives may be involved.

By the second meeting you will have sight of the franchise agreement itself. You should be allowed, and take, a reasonable period of time to study it in detail and have it reviewed by an experienced solicitor of your choice (see Chapter 3, Legal Aspects).

Only when both you and the franchisor are convinced that you wish to proceed with the contract, and are agreed that you are entering into it with all due care and preparation, should the franchise agreement or initial purchase agreement be signed.

7

Business planning

A properly run and proven franchise will almost certainly be a less risky more straightforward and planned way of going into business than setting up independently, for reasons described in Chapter 2. However, whether you can build a successful business, even with training, guidance and support from an experienced franchisor, is going to depend on the quality of all the ingredients combined in the right proportions for the venture as a whole.

Your business is more likely to be successful if it is thoroughly planned at the outset and if the plan is regularly monitored as you proceed. The business plan is for your benefit. It should take you considerable time and effort to piece it together. It is better to screw up and throw away a few pieces of paper containing plans that you realise will not work than to waste several years of your life, money and domestic harmony on ill-considered pipe-dreams.

Your franchisor should provide you with the basic information from which to build your personal plan. However, it is essential that you carry out extensive market research across your proposed territory to ensure there will be sufficient demand for the business. You will also need to analyse thoroughly your own strengths and weaknesses and how they will impact on your business plan. If premises are required, you will need to identify the optimum location, cost, size and facilities required. In retailing it is often said that the three most important secrets of success are: location, location and location!

The business plan may be described as being comprised essentially of six Ms: mission, methods, management, markets, margins and money.

Mission

Defining your mission statement forces you to identify clearly the purpose of the business. It can also be used to give an unambiguous signal of your policy and direction to others involved in your business: your financiers, employees, customers, suppliers, family and friends. It is the yardstick by which you can measure the success of the business.

Backing up the mission statement should be a clear and concise list of your objectives. The list should be 'SMART': specific, measurable, achievable, realistic and time-bound.

Methods

This means how you will organise the business, approach the market and cope with changes to the plan. This should show the organisation structure, and all the administration and recording systems you are to use. It should set out the business strategy to identify clearly how customers will be gained and retained, how the goods or services will be provided, how payment will be received and credit controlled to avoid bad debts. It should show any contingent liabilities you may incur by claims under warranties, guarantees or legal action, and how these would be dealt with. It should also include details of any restrictions placed on the business by the franchisor, such as territorial limits and the length of time granted under the franchise agreement. This section of your plan can also be used to summarise the benefits of the contract with the franchisor.

Management

Management means you and the experience, skills and knowledge you are bringing to the business. Include your age, education, and career history to date. Your profile should list details of your personal means, property, as sets, liabilities and guarantees, etc. Similar information should be recorded of any partners or fellow directors of the business. Essentially, you are analysing your own strengths and weaknesses – showing how you can capitalise and build on the strengths and how the effect of weaknesses can be minimised or substituted by the strengths of others.

Markets

This is a comprehensive term used here to describe the nature, type, make-up and size of the potential customer base, the need for your business and the route by which the customers are reached. It covers all the combined market research and resulting forecasts for sales. It should identify direct and indirect competitors, analysing their strengths and weaknesses. It should state your unique selling proposition (USP), the competitive edge by which you intend to gain market share.

The 'marketing mix' is often summarised by the four Ps: product, price, place and promotion. You should be able to describe clearly the benefits of the product, state the pricing policy, the method of distribution and selling, and determine the optimum advertising/promotional activity required.

Margins

Margins means how your business will make profits. This section should cover forecasts of sales and costings for every single anticipated expense, monthly for the first year and quarterly for the second and third years; that is, forecast trading and profit and loss statements must be shown in your business plan.

The composition of all sources of forecast income should be clearly identified. Cash sales and credit sales should be shown. Notes on the accounts should be provided to explain how every figure shown has been reached and what assumptions have been made. Rule an extra column alongside the figures that make up each month's profit forecast so that you can record actual results once you have started trading.

Your financial forecasts should include analysis of the break-even point – the point at which sales are sufficient to just cover all the costs. Break-even can be calculated by the simple formula:

$$\text{break even} = \frac{\text{overheads}}{\text{gross profit margin \%}} \times 100$$

This formula shows that the break-even point is dependent not only on the proposed gross profit, which is the difference between your selling prices and direct costs (the costs that vary directly with output) but also on total overheads (all the fixed costs that are payable irrespective of output). Any change in any of these figures forces a change in the break-even point. It is therefore wise to calculate the break-even point arising from a number of 'what-if' situations involving variations in gross margin and the anticipated overheads. Balance sheet projections may also be required.

Money

This section of your business plan covers all the funding requirements for set-up, survival, development and growth. The funding proposals should take account of your own capital investment and that of any other investors. The financial forecasts detailed under this section should cover the nature and amounts of funding required at different stages of your start-up: capital investment, long term loan and/or short-term overdraft facility, together with provisions for working capital.

You should be able to identify the specific purpose for any external funding and the length of time for which it is required. You will have to determine realistic repayment proposals to which you agree to be bound and state what security you or the business can offer as collateral.

The effects of payments out from the business against the inflow of money from sales or investment must be planned for and realised ahead of time, so a forecast cash flow analysis is essential. The cash flow forecast should be accompanied by comprehensive analysis of each figure quoted, showing how the figure is derived and qualifying every assumption that has been made.

'Profit' can mean different amounts to different people. Not only must you differentiate between gross profit and net profit, but also be aware that the Inland Revenue, investors and yourself may each allow different items to be included as costs and therefore arrive at different sums to represent overall profit. Even then, the relative figures might only become apparent after a period of time. It is cash, not profit, that pays the bills as they fall due. Many profitable businesses have collapsed for the want of immediate cash. An extra column alongside your forecast monthly cash flow figures will enable you to record actual results every month.

All of the high street banks offer excellent free information packs which can guide you clearly through the preparation of your business plan, providing you with the necessary spreadsheets, and some offer free computer disk-based formats.

NB. You must also consider what types and amounts of insurance cover you will need. It is worth taking advice from several brokers, your accountant and other business advisers.

SWOT analysis

The basis of your SWOT analysis has been described in Chapter 5. To the SWOT analysis should now be added the results of your personal profiling as assessed in Chapter 6. The overall summary of all the strengths and weaknesses inherent in your business plan, together with awareness of the opportunities and threats that could be presented to the franchise, is invaluable as a way of looking at the relative merits and pitfalls of your proposed venture and assessing the inherent risks.

Your completed business plan should be typed and several copies may be required if you are seeking funding from loans or grants. Presentation is important: your business plan should look professional if you need to have it assessed by a third party.

8

Your first franchise

Having decided to buy your first franchise and been selected by the franchisor, you should be feeling confident that you know *exactly* what you are doing. That confidence can only be achieved by thorough and painstaking research, meetings with an experienced commercial solicitor, accountant and other professional advisors, and with full backing from those close to you.

Your franchise agreement will state the maximum length of time you can take before starting your initial training programme – a period of three months is often quoted. This should allow you ample opportunity to make any necessary arrangements before your full-time commitment to the franchise begins. You may need to use the time to arrange premises, recruit staff, order equipment and prepare other facilities.

Initial training

Before signing the franchise agreement you will have arranged the dates and other details of the initial training programme for yourself, as well as for any other staff as stipulated in your franchise agreement. Initial training usually takes place at the franchisor's head office or a properly established training facility. The cost of initial training constitutes part of the initial fee; however, you will normally be responsible for any of your own further expenses, and those of any of your staff included, for items such as travel, meals and accommodation.

Your initial training programme should cover all aspects of starting up and running your own franchise. It should not be limited to just product training. The scope, depth and quality of the initial training programme can vary immensely from one franchisor to the next. You will have found out as part of your research how long the training period is and preferably will have received written confirmation of the topics to be covered and training objectives to be achieved. Your discussions with existing franchisees should have given you an idea of the quality of training to expect.

It is normal for there to be a clause in the franchise agreement that allows the franchisor to terminate the whole agreement if it becomes obvious during the initial training period that you are unlikely to succeed. This is a necessary contingency clause. Should such a circumstance arise, it is usually equally apparent to the franchisee and to his or her trainers.

Initial training usually continues into a period of supervised support within your own territory. It is in the franchisor's interests as well as your own that you should be up and running as soon as possible. You should therefore quickly be able to operate the business competently and confidently on your own, although still being able to rely on the franchisor's support, guidance and advice.

Although trading under the name and logo of the franchisor, as a franchisee you are required to state your own name and business address on all stationery, business cards, invoices etc. If operating from premises you must display a sign stating that you are operating a franchise of the business under whose name you trade.

The first few weeks and months

This period could well be one of the most nerve-racking and busy periods of your life. While you are setting about building your business perhaps you will suddenly start to worry – have you made the right decision? – are you really up to the task in hand? – why aren't sales coming in faster? If anything can go wrong with equipment or facilities, this seems to be the time that gremlins attack!

Adapting to a whole new way of life will mean changing previous living patterns. During your initial period of training, you will have relied heavily on your franchisor, but presumably your degree of satisfaction will have been quite high and you may be carrying forward the excitement of learning new skills and the enjoyment of 'being your own boss'. As you launch, all your training, knowledge, ability and support from those around you, as well as that from your franchisor, should combine to help you through this transition and well into your business plan. You will gain familiarity with the systems and methods and as your confidence grows your franchisor will have less apparent day-to-day involvement with your business, but will continue to exercise control.

The first year and beyond

In time, it is possible that you will start to resent the franchisor's continuing control, as well as having to pay the ongoing fees. You may even consider selling and opening your own independent business. If this happens, your satisfaction will reach its lowest level. It is not unknown for the occasional franchisee to seek early termination of the contract at this point, feeling that he or she has 'done it all on their own'.

As you progress with your business you will naturally become its expert in your own local territory. You may identify marketing and sales opportunities that you are not permitted to capitalise on by your franchisor, since they fall outside the range of the 'niche' market in which the franchise operates. However, it is important to remember the need for consistency across the network. Your franchisor may have a procedure that allows franchisees to contribute new ideas to the business as a whole and a framework for discussing their relative merits. Franchisees in the field cite the 'Big Mac' as an idea contributed by a McDonald's franchisee eager to increase sales ticket values and respond to customer demand.

Alternatively, franchisees may reach a 'comfort plateau' whereby they feel that they no longer have the need or desire to continue growing the business. Success can make them less competitive. The franchisor, however, naturally seeks increasing sales values since income is directly linked to turnover and the business must continue to develop in line with market trends. One of the obligations that you commit to in your franchise agreement may be to devote continuing effort to promoting and expanding your business throughout the term of your contract.

Naturally, the franchisor must stay within the bounds of the franchise agreement regarding expectations for increased sales. Those expectations may well have been represented in a model three-year forecast business plan known to you from the outset. However, one reason for a franchise agreement having a break-point at, say, the five-year stage, is to allow for modernising retail premises or replacing equipment used in the business. In order to be able to renew the contract, you may find that you are asked to expend further money on your own business facilities, to bring them into line with the latest image or resources required to keep up with market trends and customer expectations.

Successful franchise operations are often subject to 'copy cat' competition emerging rapidly to try to cash in on the market. One way of beating off such competition is for the franchisor continually to upgrade the specification of facilities available to the customer. This, of course, usually costs the franchisee further investment in fixed assets and can sometimes be a cause of dispute between franchisor and now mature franchisee.

Some conflict in the franchisee-franchisor relationship may be unavoidable, even in the best run franchise systems, particularly as the franchisee seeks to maximise profit while the franchisor is generally seeking to maximise turnover. However, debate on important issues may be encouraged by the franchisor within a franchise council or franchisee association framework.

All franchise agreements include a termination clause giving the franchisor the right to terminate the contract if the franchisee fails to adhere strictly to its terms. In practice, the franchisor can find it fairly easy to prove that the franchisee has diverged from the terms of the contract, even if only in a relatively trivial way. If the franchisor uses the threat of termination against a franchisee lightly, or at too early a stage within an apparent conflict, the franchisee's psychological need for security may not be satisfied in the long term through the franchise relationship.

On the other hand, if good communications have been fostered between the franchisor and yourself and your prime interest remains in your franchise, you will continue to recognise the importance of the franchisor's role in your success. It is through this ongoing win – win relationship that you can achieve an acceptable level of satisfaction and stability in the running of your franchise.

9
Case studies

The following case studies have been selected by the author from the finalists of the 1996 Franchisee of the Year and 1997 Franchisor of the Year competitions. These annual competitions are run by the British Franchise Association, and are sponsored by *The Express* and Midland Bank. The theme for the Franchisee of the Year Award was 'Developing your Market', while that for the Franchisor of the Year Award was 'Attracting and Retaining the Best Franchisees'.

The case studies reflect a wide range of business formats, locations, markets and franchisees. In each case a brief overview is given of the franchise, followed by the franchisees' answers to ten probing questions about their own backgrounds, experiences and observations. The franchisees who provided the case studies for the first edition of *Buying Your First Franchise* have also been 'revisited' to find out how they have fared over the last couple of years. As in the first edition of this book, franchisees and their franchisors have been extremely open, honest and straightforward in their responses. Hopefully you will find details within each case study to which you can relate, gaining further insight into franchising in practice.

Case study 1. City Link

Winners of the 1996 Franchisee of the Year Award were Bristol-based husband and wife team Richard and Kim Bird, who run their own company, Greenway Bird Express Ltd, trading as City Link (Bristol). They started their Urgent Deadlines Delivery franchise with four delivery vans in 1991, during the depth of the recession. Their business now has a turnover of £4 million, employs around 90 full-time members of staff and 15 part-timers at four sites in Bristol, Swindon, Exeter and Plymouth, operating a fleet of 55 vehicles with a capacity to handle up to 4000 items a day. Six years into their franchise, Richard and Kim have recently invested around £400,000 in extra facilities, including a new purpose-built 7000 sq ft warehouse and office complex in Bristol, adding to their existing 3000 sq ft depot there. In 1995, at their first attempt, the couple also achieved ISO 9002 accreditation for quality systems.

Commenting on their success in the Franchisee of the Year competition, Cathryn Hayes, Midland Bank's National Franchise Manager said, 'Richard and Kim have been able to fund further franchise acquisitions through growth – to successfully "Develop their Market". They have an impressive track record and are without doubt truly deserving winners.'

Richard and Kim were presented with the top award, along with a cheque for £5000, by the Head of Business Banking at Midland. They also received a commemorative plate which was presented by Sir Bernard Ingham, President of the British Franchise Association, on behalf of the sponsors Midland Bank and *The Express*.

Kim responded very positively to the following questions:

Q.1 Why did you become franchisees?

Richard had been in business with two partners, engaged in computerised typesetting, but many customers were starting to acquire desk top publishing facilities and we could see that our business opportunities were declining. Richard had always been interested in transport and was naturally drawn towards the idea of moving into the parcel carrier business. We sold the typesetting business to an existing large customer and explored the parcels market. We liked the idea of having a lot of autonomy, yet with the network and support a franchise offers. City Link offered a strong Agreement; we could run our own business, making our own decisions, but with the reassurance that we were not on our own.

Talking to existing City Link franchisees showed us how they kept up with trends in the market and were able to rate their individual performances in it through league tables produced by the franchisor. It was obvious that the network was successful. Bristol is Richard's home town and we were able to buy the franchise there, moving home to do so.

Q.2 What were your occupations before taking up the franchise, and what knowledge or skills have been useful to you in the business?

Richard's experience in the previous business was useful and he had always been involved in sales and management. I had received secretarial training and had experience of that sort of work, including bookkeeping, credit control and reception duties. I kept the accounts for the typesetting business and also had a spell as a self-employed bookkeeper/secretary for other small firms in the area, using a Sage Accounting computer package. I think our 'people skills' have been most useful, and these have been developed much more by the franchise. We are both very thorough in everything we do.

Q.3 How well prepared for self-employment were you before taking up the franchise?

Fairly well; Richard more so. We knew the formalities and thought we were used to dealing with people. Even so, we went up a steep learning curve in how to deal with different sorts of people. As a couple we had not worked together before, so I think we were both a bit cautious about that. In the event, we each have our own responsibilities within the business and find that it works well. We enjoy sharing the experience and both have a sense of equal ownership.

Q.4 What are your longer-term aims and ambitions?

We've worked long and hard for six years now, but we're getting there. We plan to have a stronger management structure. Richard is 52 and so we have set ourselves at least another eight years to build up the business, when we can then perhaps part-retire. We have two sons, aged 19 and 17, neither of whom at the moment show particular interest in taking over the business. Our elder son is more ambitious in the field of IT.

Q.5 What attracted you to the City Link franchise?

The Agreement. It suited us; it gave us a lot of scope to run our own business, handle our own accounts etc, so there were better margins than when the franchisor handles that side of the business, and we had the experience to deal with it. We were able to employ our own people and sales methods. In fact we had originally planned to buy a different franchise but it fell through at the last moment, so I think fate also had a lot to do with it!

Q.6 Has the business performed to your expectations?

Yes! Very much so. We have put a lot of money into it and we had to learn a lot about the parcel business. For the first six months or so we factored our invoices and that helped enormously with cash flow. We were then in a position to handle our own credit control and obtain the better margin from doing that. We have always reinvested back into the business and it continues to perform well.

Q.7 What disappointments or let-downs have you experienced?

The parcels business is very instant. If there is a problem, we react instantly; that way problems get dealt with and don't grow out of proportion. When we were just 18 months into the business, we had a bad debt for £12,000 but that sharpened us up in our dealings and our credit control, including the credit we allowed for new customers. There have been no disappointments with the franchise itself.

Q.8 How would you describe your franchisor, and how would you rate the training, advice and support you have received so far?

'Very good. City Link is part of the Rentokil Initial Group, which ranks 30th in the UK's top 100 companies. They invest a lot in training their own staff as well as franchisees, so back-up is good and professional.'

Q.9 Has being a franchisee changed either of you in any way?

Being successful is great. We are more confident and able to deal with problems – we take them in our stride. I find that I am much more assertive now. Even recently I surprised myself over how well I negotiated the purchase of my mother's new car.

Q.10 What advice would you offer to someone thinking of buying their first franchise?

Definitely be interested in the business itself. If you are a couple, then both should share that interest. Talk to other franchisees in the network. Explore the field. Find a Franchise Agreement that is strong for you. I would always recommend choosing a member of the British Franchise Association, so you know they have signed up to the BFA Code of Ethics.

Case study 2. Saks Hairdressing

Winner of the second prize in the 1996 Franchisee of the Year competition and receiving a cheque for £3,000 was Wilson Derbyshire, franchisee for Saks (Hair). Wilson now runs three Saks salons, having bought his first franchise in Northallerton in May 1991 at the age of 21, and has since expanded into Newcastle-upon-Tyne and Scunthorpe, with a fourth salon opening in Harrogate in October

1997. Wilson is single and operates as a sole trader, but has gone into partnership with the previous owner of the Scunthorpe salon to develop that site along with the one planned for Harrogate. He now employs 35 full-time staff and has gained an enviable reputation within the Saks network, having won their 'Salon of the Year' Award in 1994 and again in 1996, making him the only salon owner to have won this accolade twice.

Midland Bank's National Franchise Manager commented on Wilson's achievement in the 1996 Franchisee of the Year competition, 'Wilson has developed his marketing innovatively. When starting out in business he chose the Saks franchise because the group had in place a definite career structure, which has enabled him to achieve his goal. He is a perfect role model, illustrating the level of success which can be achieved by using a proven business format franchising formula. Also, along with building up a substantial business with great enthusiasm, Wilson has managed to raise in excess of £40,000 for local charities in his area and that alone is a major achievement.'

Wilson was enthusiastic in his answers to the questions put to him:

Q.1 Why did you become a franchisee?

I trained with Saks, starting on the YTS scheme at 16. From my apprenticeship with an existing Saks franchisee I became a stylist, then senior stylist, and then went on to become Assistant Manager in the franchised salon, so I knew how they worked. I did try to go independent by myself when I was 20–21, but I had no track record and found it very difficult to get a lease on suitable premises, and it was hard to raise funds from the banks.

Q.2 What was your occupation before taking up the franchise, and what knowledge or skills have been useful to you in the business?

Having been trained by Saks I was in their 'culture' already and was encouraged to follow a definite career path and training which could lead to owning your own salon. It enabled me to make mistakes, but not at my own expense!

Q.3 How well prepared for self-employment were you before taking up the franchise?

I was well prepared. I took it on at 21 – the Saks culture is team based but very competitive and teaches you how to win. My parents were self-employed, so I was used to that way of life.

Q.4 What are your longer-term aims and ambitions?

I am now 28. I want to build an equity base and perhaps move into a Regional Directorship role within the Saks Group, while still retaining my own salons. This idea has already been discussed with Saks management and could become a possibility. I would like to be in the position of owning the freeholds of salon properties, or building my own. I fancy being the landlord and having a passive income.

Q.5 What attracted you to the Saks franchise?

For me it was the 'culture'. I had followed the career path and was committed to the ethos; I knew Saks were too. It's like a large family, with a tremendous team spirit. It's for young people and we don't respond well to 'suits'! Saks empower their franchisees, building successful teams. There are franchisee working parties and the whole company is energetic. I felt I could do it, that I belonged, and the marketing and financial package were right.

Q.6 Has the business performed to your expectations?

To them and beyond. Saks has grown and I have grown. This year the industry as a whole is up by 8 per cent on last year; Saks is up by 22 per cent; my business is up 38 per cent on last year.

Q.7 What disappointments or let-downs have you experienced?

Landlords. Sometimes large property firms still don't take you seriously and are not as flexible as you would like. I have a problem which has been rumbling on for a long time now where the property landlord will not allow me to expand to the next floor of the building, so my salon there is restricted for space. After about two years as a franchisee I did overstretch my cash flow. It was my own fault because I did not heed advice from the Saks management and it did cause a problem at the time. However, they were still very helpful and gave me further advice, but I then suddenly realised that it really was down to me to make it work and I think that experience did me some good.

Q.8 How would you describe your franchisor, and how would you rate the training, advice and support you have received so far?

I have looked at other similar businesses, but Saks are the market leaders. Their management training is brilliant. They have the right people teaching the right things. The technical training is very, very good. I understand that Saks are the largest account for L'Oreal products and the staff training and product support are great. I like going on the courses. The training goes well beyond the basics.

Q.9 Has being a franchisee changed you in any way?

Yes! I used to be successful at the expense of everyone else, but I've learned that win/win is much better. Hairdressing is ego-based and that is hard to get around when you are trying to build teams. Now I am proud when one of my staff achieves something special and I encourage them into the spotlight.

Q.10 What advice would you offer to someone thinking of buying their first franchise?

In hairdressing, look beyond the name and the image and see *exactly* what is on offer. Contact the franchisor and, more importantly, their franchisees. Look for commitment to the craft. You want excellent products and systems that are well thought out. Go for a franchisor who runs company-owned outlets as well as having franchised ones, and preferably is the market leader. Look for back-up and good communications. Saks hold regular quarterly meetings and the franchisees have a strong sense of ownership.

In recognition of their ability to 'Attract and Retain the Best Franchisees' the parent company Saks Hair (Holdings) Ltd also won the 1997 Midland Bank Award for their outstanding dedication and consistency in the level of support they give their franchisees.

Case study 3. Greenalls Inn Partnership

Third prize winner in the 1996 Franchisee of the Year Awards were husband and wife partnership Jean and John Taylor, who received a cheque for £2000. At the time of the competition, Jean and John had run The Derby Arms at Inskip, near Preston, Lancashire, since February 1993. In January 1996 they moved on to also pilot a major new franchise format for Greenalls pubs, while their son Ian manages The Derby Arms. Their latest challenge, though, is far more than an average pub – even by Greenalls standards.

The White Crow at Worthington, near Wigan, includes a 120-cover restaurant serving a whole range of interesting meals, a barbeque, gardens and a menagerie of pet goats, sheep and rabbits to keep the children amused. At The Derby Arms son Ian has also taken over the care of the pigs, ducks, rabbits and geese!

Between them, Jean and John have won a lot of awards because of their high standards, and these have led to excellent local PR and a lot of publicity. Jean is now also called upon by Greenalls to work for them on a daily fee rate as a Business Partner Training Adviser. Jean and John employ 7 full- and 33 part-time staff. John reigns supreme in the kitchens, while Jean manages the front of house.

John decided that Jean was better at answering the questions and she did so very openly.

Q.1 Why did you become franchisees?

To make profit for ourselves after years of making money for others in managed houses. We were used to working hard, and running your own business means your rewards are directly in line with your efforts. Franchising gave us that possibility.

Q.2 What were your occupations before taking up the franchise, and what knowledge or skills have been useful to you in the business?

John was an apprentice chef for five years and a Head Chef at the age of 22. I used my BTec in Business and Finance to do accounts for other businesses while John was 'chefing'. From the age of 18, I was a nanny for five years with one family. John and I then married and I worked in a Special Care Baby Unit. I've worked part-time in pubs and restaurants since I was 14 years of age, when waitresses wore long skirts and the men were in tails for silver service. At 16, I was doing VAT returns. John and I have known each other since those teenage years and we are now celebrating our Silver Wedding anniversary.

Q.3 How well prepared for self-employment were you before taking up the franchise?

We had both been in the trade, therefore we knew we had the skills and could take on the responsibility for ourselves. We have always been frugal and used to a minimum wage, so we were not taking a step backwards financially while waiting for the business to build. Also, our social life is the pub, so that fitted as well. We both had developed 'people skills'. I was a nanny at 18, responsible not only for the children but also for an undermaid, a gardener and a housekeeper. We were both used to managing people older than ourselves, although John is much more of a 'doer' than a delegator. Staff tend to confide in John more than me as he is very approachable and perhaps more readily seen as 'one of them'.

Q.4 What are your longer-term aims and ambitions?

More pubs. We hope to pass on the businesses to our sons. Ian is aged 23 and manages The Derby Arms at Inskip for us. Duncan, 20, is following in his father's footsteps as a chef and also learning office skills. We want to be the best at what we do. Greenalls have two examples of a new type of larger pub undergoing pilot testing and The White Crow is one of them. It calls for a higher level of investment, typically £70,000–£100,000, but we are proud of being given this opportunity to pioneer the scheme.

Q.5 What attracted you to Greenalls?

Training. Greenalls only franchise pubs. It's a bridge between freehold and managed premises, and you get all the back-up of a big firm. They are very friendly and you can see the Managing Director at any time if you wish; they are not 'stand-offish', but it is entirely up to you as to how much you want to get involved.

Q.6 Has the business performed to your expectations?

Yes. Our first three years were excellent, but then we were affected by the closure of HMS Inskip when the Navy moved out. These days there is also a lot more local competition for people's leisure time and it's a lot harder to 'pack them in'; shops are open longer hours and on Sundays, so the pattern of trade has shifted.

Q.7 What disappointments or let-downs have you experienced?

The closure of HMS Inskip affected the whole village. We had enjoyed a good relationship with the Navy. The Inskip area is designated green belt, so there is no growth in the local youth population. John organises a lot of youth activities and likes doing that. The activities are nothing to do with drinking of course, but we are part of the community and help where we can.

There have been no disappointments or let-downs at all from Greenalls. They come round to do a monthly check and help in discussing the business, so potential problems are quickly picked up. There is good feedback on marketing trends.

Q.8 How would you describe your franchisor, and how would you rate the training, advice and support you have received so far?

Excellent training. Quick support. There's always advice at the end of the telephone. I remember one occasion when we were really bogged down, very busy. The physical support we received was immediate – and much welcomed! You get a lot of encouragement, awards and praise. There are staff awards too and lots of courses for them – craft courses, management courses, NVQs and so on. Greenalls run a programme called Gateways, which gives any member of the staff the opportunity to then be offered their own tenancy on good terms if they also have the financial backing needed.

Q.9 Has being a franchisee changed you in any way?

I would say we are both more independent and more ambitious now. We never turn down work and have become more multi-skilled and adaptable. John used to be more of a back room person, but now he is much more at the front. He is a character in his own right, popular and has lots of confidence. It's his own kingdom.

Q.10 What advice would you offer to someone thinking of buying their first franchise?

Look at the site and location. Ask yourself what it is that you have got to do to fulfil that franchise? Go on courses, learn. Talk to existing franchisees, see if they are successful or despondent. Is the business really what you want? Are you disciplined enough? Is it what customers want? Is the franchisor up to date? Don't ever be complacent, be like a chameleon and change with every situation.

Case study 4. Pirtek

Pirtek won the 1997 Franchisor of the Year Award. The company provides specialist on-site hydraulic services and has grown steadily since its inception in 1989 so that it now has 62 wholly-owned franchise centres in the UK, with an overall network turnover of £23 million. Pirtek also recently finalised a Master Licence for the US where trading has already commenced in Minneapolis, successfully replicating 'over there' the UK proven format.

To represent Pirtek, the author chose one of their Scottish franchisees. Eric MacKenzie runs his own limited company, Graphbury Ltd, which has traded as Pirtek (Glasgow) since November 1992 and is proving highly successful for him. Eric started with three vans to cover all his Glasgow territory. He now runs three Transits and two Mercedes 412D vehicles, with a further vehicle on order. Fully equipped and stocked, each Transit represents around £25,000 investment, while the larger 7.5 tonnes gross weight Mercedes are worth around £40,000 each. Eric's business keeps nine full-time employees busy, operating shop and mobile services from retail and industrial warehousing in Glasgow. Eric's business recently received the highest accolade in Pirtek as winner of their Best Centre Award, chosen from amongst all of Pirtek's 62 centres throughout the UK.

Eric's is a 'one-man' limited company, he enjoys the business side of the work and he was open and forthright in his anwers to the questions:

Q.1 Why did you become a franchisee?

To be in business for myself. I felt able to do it. Originally I was looking at Pirtek as a possible add-on to a much larger operation, the Perkins Diesel franchise for Scotland. However, when I really examined it I decided it would be a much simpler business to operate as it stood. It was quicker, that is it drew on a much higher volume of customers who would pay more quickly than perhaps a few larger customers would. It also showed better margins to be gained. It was a similar customer/consumer base to the Perkins business, so I felt comfortable with the market.

Q.2 What was your occupation before taking up the franchise, and what knowledge or skills have been useful to you in the business?

I had run a business as a manager for the Perkins Diesel franchisee in Scotland. My experience in managing that business was of course very useful.

Q.3 How well prepared for self-employment were you before taking up the franchise?

Not very well! On a scale of one to ten, I would say I rated about six, which is quite poor. Having resigned my job, I was up and running within six weeks, though, so there wasn't much time to think about that. I had a lot of help from Pirtek, particularly in finding suitable premises. But I got the initial staff almost entirely wrong! I must admit it all seemed a lot easier on paper than it was in real life. Other people just don't have the same commitment as you do.

Q.4 What are your longer-term aims and ambitions?

In the medium term it is to maintain things much as they are, but I do anticipate doubling my turnover and profit. I may consider buying out other existing franchisees. As for the long term – South of France? Gulf of Mexico?

Q.5 What attracted you to Pirtek?

The concept appealed to me. I had seen the gap in the market, although I hadn't thought of exploiting it as a mobile service. I saw an advertisement and could see myself doing it. I liked the name. I didn't have enough money, but managed it with a huge mortgage and a good banker!

Q.6 Has the business performed to your expectations?

Although I met sales targets in the first year, and the gross margin was right, I made a loss which was larger than expected for Year One. It was my own fault really, I carried higher stock than recommended, paid higher salaries, had more staff etc. It did make me very stretched financially, and my own mental performance was affected. Two to three years later and it was OK. The business has been profitable since Year Two and is now really making it, with lots of potential.

Q.7 What disappointments or let-downs have you experienced?

That first year cash flow was bad and I had staff problems. I had to take steps to put on paper the full details of what I expected. You need staff who are trustworthy and reliable. The staff I have now are as good as any you can get and morale is good. In 1996 I had a bad debt for £7000, but the business was strong enough to weather the storm.

Q.8 How would you describe your franchisor, and how would you rate the training, advice and support you have received so far?

The support and commitment from Pirtek has been exceptional. They helped me see through the initial financial problems, and it is very much a two-way relationship. I've checked out other firms, at exhibitions and so on and talked with franchisees from other systems, but I'm convinced there's none to compare.

Q.9 Has being a franchisee changed you in any way?

Being in business, I'm more sceptical about taking on board people's verbal promises, especially where money is involved. I don't fly by the seat of my pants any more. I'm more confident in myself. My wife was partly involved in the business at the start, but family life is away from the business.

Q.10 What advice would you offer to someone thinking of buying their first franchise?

I think I've been lucky. I would advise that they look at the track record. Go and visit existing franchisees. Check the area/territory size and composition. Do their own local market research. Don't underestimate the need for working capital – even though I might have been frightened off if I had known! Be out selling, rather than in a shop – you have more control. Have a sales plan and segment the market. I felt comfortable with the Pirtek people – they looked like quality people who had done their homework.

Case study 5. Rainbow International

Representing Wales in these case studies is 28-year-old Huw Smith, who runs the very successful Rainbow International franchise in Cardiff and Swansea. Rainbow International specialise in carpet and upholstery cleaning and repair, carpet dyeing and flood or fire restoration for commercial and domestic customers.

Huw was a finalist in the 1996 Franchisee of the Year competition even though he had only started his business in September 1994. As a sole trader, he now employs nine full-time employees and eight part-timers, some of whom are mobile, while others work within his 5000 sq ft warehouse, where he also carries out a great deal of off-site cleaning, restoration and storage.

Huw responded confidently to the questions:

Q.1 Why did you become a franchisee?

I had run my own carpet cleaning business for two years, just myself in a van, but I wanted to get into the much larger and more regular insurance-based market. I needed to expand the business, to employ people in a more secure environment. A loss adjuster put me on to the franchise idea, since a network can provide insurance companies with the service their customers need.

Q.2 What was your occupation before taking up the franchise, and what knowledge or skills have been useful to you in the business?

My skill and technical knowledge from my own carpet cleaning business were useful. Before I started my own small business, I was Domestic Services Manager for the Henley Management Centre, so I had some experience in management. I had also run a hotel in France for six months, using my HND qualification in that line of work.

Q.3 How well prepared for self-employment were you before taking up the franchise?

I had a Business Studies OND and some management experience, but I hadn't run a large operation as my own business before.

Q.4 What are your longer-term aims and ambitions?

This year my business will top £½ million turnover and there is more work to get. I could diversify, into decorating for example. By the time I'm 35 or 40 I want to be doing other things, such as travel, sport – I like golf – and generally having more time off.

Q.5 What attracted you to Rainbow International?

As in my answer to your first question, a loss adjuster put me on to it – the firm has a good, sound reputation in the industry. They are an international company, and the people I spoke to there were honest and sincere, committed to their business.

Q.6 Has the business performed to your expectations?

More than I expected. I was turning over £20,000 on my own, expecting maybe £25,000 by my third year. I have grown this business to half a million pounds in two-and-a-half years.

Q.7 What disappointments or let-downs have you experienced?

There have been no disappointments. In my head I suppose I'd imagined there might have been more national contracts, like shop chains perhaps, but I'm very happy with what I'm doing.

Q.8 How would you describe your franchisor, and how would you rate the training, advice and support you have received so far?

The training and advice have been very good and the support is continuous. They are committed to the business and encourage the franchisees to generate more business. Their training courses for staff are good and they are committed to helping any franchisee who is similarly committed to helping himself and his business. We have a good relationship.

Q.9 Has being a franchisee changed you in any way?

Yes. I'm more interested in marketing and turnover than in the equipment now. I used to spend a lot of time thinking about the equipment, looking inwards. Now I'm working *on* the business, not *in* the business.

Q.10 What advice would you offer to someone thinking of buying their first franchise?

Check that it is a viable proposition. Look behind the glitz and the glamour, especially what you see at exhibitions. Check the territory and do your own local market research. Talk to existing franchisees, find out how they have grown. Can you diversify? If you want to be able to diversify, there should be no restrictions.

Case study 6. ServiceMaster

Also finalists in the 1996 Franchisee of the Year competition were husband and wife partnership John and Julia Foad from Ashford in Kent. John and Julia began their ServiceMaster franchise in January 1990 when John retired from his career in the Army after 25 years' service, having reached the rank of Major.

ServiceMaster is also in the cleaning business, but differs from the previous case study in some of the markets which it targets. John and Julia do not provide the ServiceMaster contract cleaning service, preferring to concentrate on on-location cleaning and repairs for furnishings in homes and offices, as well as providing French polishing services. They also undertake work referred from insurers. For the home cleaning services, Julia runs the Merry Maid franchise from ServiceMaster. The couple operate from offices in their 3500 sq ft industrial unit, with a further 200 sq ft unit nearby. They employ seven full-time and four part-time staff.

John was very helpful in answering the questions about themselves and their experience:

Q.1 Why did you become franchisees?

I was retiring from the services and decided it would be a fairly easy step. You don't have to reinvent the wheel. There is network support and we knew that, compared with independent start-ups, a higher proportion of franchises succeed. The franchise would also give us the contacts and enable us to work with national contracts.

Q.2 What was your occupation before taking up the franchise, and what knowledge or skills have been useful to you in the business?

I was an Army Major, an avionics engineer completing my 25 years' signing. After my trade apprenticeship I was commissioned and was a Major for the final three years. That taught me about man management, survival, being flexible and adaptable, and harnessing drive and initiative. Julia had run her own wool shop and her parents ran their own successful business. She had also run an accounts department for a local firm during the 1970s and had taught computer studies. Julia was first interested in the Merry Maids franchise and she went to the US to see how it worked, piloting it in the UK when she returned.

Q.3 How well prepared for self-employment were you before taking up the franchise?

We felt confident. We knew we were good at motivating people – we had no skills in selling but felt confident at communicating. Of course, a commission in the Army teaches you to deal with all sorts of problems and how to manage crises. It also teaches standards and punctuality etc.

Q.4 What are your longer-term aims and objectives?

We do tend to live for the business now. Our son Matthew joined it last October and I think we are looking to long-term security. Frankly, it's just nice to be home in England; we've done all the travelling around while I was in the Army – all over the world – so we like having roots now.

Q.5 What attracted you to ServiceMaster?

We analysed what was on offer, saw the insurance market could be developed and so targeted that market. The recession was starting and ServiceMaster appeared to be the only ones penetrating that market. We are used to crisis management and felt we could cope with dealing with flood and fire damage etc. Having standards – and just being punctual – is a big plus in this service industry.

Q.6 Has the business performed to your expectations?

Yes. In fact it has expanded at a far quicker rate than we expected, or were led to believe. The original estimates from ServiceMaster proved to be conservative and they had certainly erred on the side of caution, predicting only about 75 per cent of what we actually achieved. Although that was to their credit for the first year, it meant we faced cash flow problems in our second year! The business was outstripping our ability to keep it going, growing by a further 60 per cent in that second year. After that it settled down and has grown thereafter at a rate of about 20 per cent each year.

Q.7 What disappointments or let-downs have you experienced?

It's hard to think of any. The insurance market is safe, even though you have to wait a while for payment. We knew it would be hard work, so that was no surprise. One carpet manufacturer we dealt with went bust, but we lost only £600.

Q.8 How would you describe your franchisor, and how would you rate the training, advice and support you have received so far?

We have looked across the market and they seem to be one of the better ones around. There can always be shortcomings, maybe glitches when there are changes to systems etc, but we are happy to pay the royalties. I remember when our leather expert went into hospital with appendicitis, ServiceMaster provided the technical help we needed.

Q.9 Has being a franchisee changed you in any way?

I don't know. I suppose I could have become more of a crotchety and crusty old major, but you have to show sympathy for customers whose possessions have suffered flood or fire damage. Julia and I work together, but apart, as we each have our own responsibilities in the business. It is a nice lifestyle.

Q.10 What advice would you offer to someone thinking of buying their first franchise?

Speak to and visit other franchisees. Pick out the ones you want to talk with, don't just accept ones suggested by the franchisor. Look at the performance spectrum of all franchisees in the system. There is also one thing I advise anybody in business – answer the phone!

Case study 7. Molly Maid

Still with the cleaning business, but providing a professional domestic maid service, is Sandra Redmond of Wimbledon. Sandra runs her own limited company, Halestrong Ltd, trading as Molly Maid (Wimbledon), in which she employs 20 full-time staff working from eight cars and turning over a quarter of a million pounds a year. Sandra was also proud to be selected as a finalist in the 1996 Franchisee of the Year competition, even though she had bought the business from a previous franchisee only one year before.

Sandra was pleased to answer the questions put to her:

Q.1 Why did you become a franchisee?

A friend of mine owned the franchise and it's what I call being a soft entrepreneur. I like having parameters and guidelines and I saw it as a formula for success. I knew I had the ability to grow an existing idea, rather than try to invent one myself.

Q.2 What was your occupation before taking up the franchise, and what knowledge or skills have been useful to you in the business?

I was a Load Development Engineer in the marketing department of Seeboard – South East Electricity. I was used to customer relations, presentations, 'interfacing' with people (although I don't like that word!). People skills are very important and this business is all about matching people to clients to provide a bespoke service.

Q.3 How well prepared for self-employment were you before taking up the franchise?

Financially I had received a severance sum from my employer. I think I was lucky. I was used to working on my own and have always been self-motivated, so the next step was easier, although it didn't have a pay cheque attached and at the time I did feel I was paying for a job. Every minute of the day has to be productive. I had no knowledge of accounts but knew I had to justify every penny. I also had good support from my partner.

Q.4 What are your longer-term aims and ambitions?

Stability to retirement. I think that money 'happens'. I would like to be known as the best and be recognised for being a good business woman, a sort of role model.

Q.5 What attracted you to Molly Maid?

My friend. I recognised the name and the livery. My friend worked hard and the franchise was for everybody and it particularly helps other women. I respect and admire Pam Bader, who runs the company. There is a feeling of belonging and it was nice to know it was there.

Q.6 Has the business performed to your expectations?

Yes. I expected a job, but it fulfils the parts of me that were never used at Seeboard – and I thought I would be happy to just jog along! The income is good and yes, it has exceeded my expectations.

Q.7 What disappointments or let-downs have you experienced?

You get let down by people – clients and employees. You have to rely on yourself 100 per cent and I have had to build loyalty from my employees; for example they now know they can't just say they are taking a day off whenever they like.

Q.8 How would you describe your franchisor, and how would you rate the training, advice and support you have received so far?

As I was taking over an existing business I felt I had to throw myself into it straight away. I had to quickly get to know my customers, rather than build the business step by step. Of what I have used from the company, I have found them very supportive and nurturing. It was reassuring just knowing that they were there if I needed them. We have a good two-way dialogue now that life runs more smoothly and I can enjoy my time. They put on really good training days, on employment law, for example.

Q.9 Has being a franchisee changed you in any way?

I am more discerning and objective, forming my own opinions. I am more even tempered now, but I don't assume anything and am certainly more assertive. I have learned to say no! I think women are taught to say yes, but I won't accept shoddy work, especially from advertising companies.

Q.10 What advice would you offer to someone thinking of buying their first franchise?

Look into it and be very, very careful. Speak to as many people as you can and as many franchisees as possible. Make sure that the name is everything it stands for. Ask yourself if you really want to do it, will you enjoy it?

Case study 8. Prontaprint

One of the two franchisees working in fast print, copy, and design who won a place in the final of the 1996 Franchisee of the Year competition was Andrew Murdoch. Andrew has owned the Prontaprint franchise in Barking, Essex as a sole trader since 1983. Andrew's wife, Wendy, does some of the bookkeeping and they have been married for 26 years. The franchise is now very much a business-to-business service, rather than retail driven, and Andrew employs nine full-time staff at his well-established commercial unit.

Andrew was very positive in his answers to the range of questions asked:

Q.1 Why did you become a franchisee?

I had been in print as a machine salesman. Redundancy started the thought process that I might set up on my own. Some of my former customers ran print/copy/design shops so I knew how they operated and saw at first hand the support franchisees received. I also heard franchisees' comments about the excellent support they received if they had technical problems, for example. I had always liked the Prontaprint format, so it was natural that I should talk with them. I felt that Prontaprint would add to my own development.

Q.2 What was your occupation before taking up the franchise, and what knowledge or skills have been useful to you in the business?

As a print machine salesman I had selling and management experience. I had determination and was prepared to work hard. I had a good knowledge of print and machinery. Although I was used to selling much higher priced goods, I found I still got a buzz from achieving the lower price-ticket sales within Prontaprint. I was used to working with people and motivating them.

Q.3 How well prepared for self-employment were you before taking up the franchise?

I had no experience in employing people and no experience of accounting. I had always had the benefit of a salary, plus commission; I was never commission only. I took to being self-employed like a duck to water.

Q.4 What are your longer-term aims and ambitions?

For the business, it is to grow and generate more profit. My business hours are 8.45am to 5.15pm, but I generally work 12 hours a day, often including Saturdays and Sundays. As a couple, we hope to have more time for each other, but I'm looking to the business continuing for the next ten years.

Q.5 What attracted you to Prontaprint?

I was comfortable with print and with Prontaprint.

Q.6 Has the business performed to your expectations?

Yes – and no. Overall the business has done well, but in 1991 the recession was biting and also there were a lot of changes made to Barking town centre. The retail premises I had at the time became the only shop left open along that road.

Q.7 What disappointments or let-downs have you experienced?

The recession. The changes made by the council to the town centre. I do like to continually try new things, so there are the occasional disappointments – but I still like to have a go!

Q.8 How would you describe your franchisor, and how would you rate the training, advice and support you have received so far?

Very good. We have a good relationship and a good two-way exchange. You need to take part in order to get value out, so it is a matter of participation. I am currently trying out a new format for Prontaprint. It is a business unit, not a retail shop. I do get good support if I need it. In my 14 years' experience as a Prontaprint franchisee I have found the staff training good, although at one point it did become rather variable.

Q.9 Has being a franchisee changed you in any way?

I am more rounded in nature than I was. It has opened me up to a wider spread of experience. Although I am still the salesman, I am no longer 'salesman selfish'.

Q.10 What advice would you offer to someone thinking of buying their first franchise?

Do something you enjoy – it's a lot easier to be motivated. Franchising is no excuse for not working hard. Deal with a franchise that has a track record. Talk to existing franchisees. Make sure the franchisor is not out for a quick buck. Look to the BFA for guidance. Remember, the franchisor will not provide you with a living. You need to feel happy about taking responsibility for that yourself, and be confident in your own abilities. Being a franchisee means that you still need that spark of personal motivation.

Case study 9. Kall Kwik

The last case study arising from the 1996 Franchisee of the Year competition are husband and wife finalists Terry and Marcelle Woods who, as Starchoice Services Ltd, run the successful Kall Kwik fast print, copy and design franchise in Chiswick, London. They took up the franchise in May 1984 and operate from a retail outlet providing business-to-business services with the help of their 16 full-time and two part-time employees.

Terry volunteered to respond to the questions and provided an excellent insight into the couple's 13 years in franchising:

Q.1 Why did you become franchisees?

We were previously running our own business and wanted to stay our own boss, but also wanted the support of a larger company.

Q.2 What was your occupation before taking up the franchise, and what knowledge or skills have been useful to you in the business?

We were in retailing, running our own two greengrocery shops. Knowing the disciplines needed to run our own business was useful. Marcelle had also been a senior administrator in a Japanese pharmaceutical company and therefore possessed skills on that side of the business and is very methodical.

Q.3 How well prepared for self-employment were you before taking up the franchise?

We were OK as far as self-employment was concerned, but the greengrocery had been a simple cash business. We were not used to the complexities of running a much larger business and invoicing customers etc. At the start we used to say that our biggest supplier was the bank!

Q.4 What are your longer-term aims and ambitions?

We are not looking for any further outlets – there's still enough for us in Chiswick. At 45–46 years of age we are looking to continue for the next 10 years. We have our pension planned, so we are looking for capital growth as well as income. There is the thought that as Kall Kwik looks for individuals to buy into the franchise it could become harder for us, as the value of our business increases, to find the buyer needed to provide us with our exit route – success brings its own problems!

Q.5 What attracted you to Kall Kwik?

Going back 13 years, there was not the range and diversity of franchises there is today – it was really fast food or print – and we did not want to be in the fast food business. Kall Kwik appeared professional, aggressive and outgoing, which suited us and continues to do so.

Q.6 Has the business performed to your expectations?

Back then it did take much longer to become profitable than we thought it would. It was five years before we started to see substantial profit. The first year ran at a substantial loss, the second and third years incurred smaller losses, but Year Four showed a small profit. Since then it has grown and we haven't looked back.

Q.7 What disappointments or let-downs have you experienced?

We were disappointed in the first five years and it was out of kilter with the original plan. In business you do have set-backs, you lose good staff etc.

Q.8 How would you describe your franchisor, and how would you rate the training, advice and support you have received so far?

Ethical. Their only income stream is from franchisees and you are not forced to buy supplies from the company. The training was always good, now it is excellent. There are heavily subsidised courses for all franchisees and staff, run regionally.

Q.9 Has being a franchisee changed you in any way?

When we started up, I ran the business until Marcelle left her job and joined it after about six months. It has made us both more confident. We have a substantial business and have become very successful at dealing with other substantial firms – we can now challenge them to give us their business.

Q.10 What advice would you offer to someone thinking of buying their first franchise?

As far as Kall Kwik is concerned, that is easy to answer as the company often do send prospective new franchisees to see us. We always advise them to invest in people before investing in machinery and equipment, to keep staff well motivated, well paid and well looked after, to develop their feeling of worth to the business. We have one person who has been with us 12 years now. Having left school with no qualifications, he now runs our entire printing department. Running the franchise has been enormously hard work and for the first three years everything else was on hold.

The individuals who provided case studies for the first edition of *Buying Your First Franchise* were contacted again and invited to share their experiences since that time. Each was asked whether there had been any major changes to their business since their responses to the original 1995 questions and, if so, what had they been and had they been expected. They were also asked whether their business had improved or declined and, if so, by how much it had changed. Finally, they were asked if they still believed that taking up the franchise had been the right course for them, and whether they had any regrets.

First to be 'revisited' was Mike Slee who, with his two partners, has run the Autosmart franchise around the Southampton area of the south coast since 1992. Mike reported that the business has stabilised, is just as busy, but going from strength to strength. They are consolidating their sales accounts and the market itself has stabilised. There are now fewer competitors, with a lot of the one-man-with-a-van enterprises having gone. There are still some of the more established individuals left, but the competition is now mostly made up of the larger firms.

Mike's business has grown by around 15 per cent since 1995 and he is convinced that the franchise was the right choice for him and his two partners. They still receive excellent back-up from Autosmart, although they do not now need to call upon the company for as much support as in their early days.

Andrew and Pat Preskett realised the capital value of their 'Circle C' convenience store in Goring by Sea by selling it in July 1996. The Circle C franchise system now operates under the Alldays banner, having been acquired by Alldays at the end of 1994, and the Goring store is now owned by another franchisee who bought it as a going concern.

In the first edition of *Buying Your First Franchise* there were three examples of the Molly Maid franchise. Ernest and Pat Torrence had started theirs in Edinburgh in 1994, at the same time as Diana Midgley was launching hers in Wetherby. Janet Dunn had been running her Molly Maid franchise from her home in South London since 1991. All three franchises are still operating successfully, although Janet sold hers after exactly five years, moving house at the same time.

Ernest and Pat reported that their business has grown by 47 per cent since the 1995 questionnaire. They now run six cars (two Maids per car) compared with the three they had operated before, and they have graduated to the Molly Maid 'President's Circle'. They have improved communications within their business and their staff are now all equipped with pagers or mobile telephones, helping them run the business more efficiently. They have no regrets whatever about their franchise, although they do find it hard to get good, reliable staff. They were due to fly off to Canada to visit their younger son out there – it was he who had taken them to the 1993 National Franchise Exhibition at the NEC Birmingham and first introduced them to the idea of franchising. This was to be their second holiday in six months, their first having been a marvellous trip to Goa in India.

Diana Midgley's Molly Maid franchise has likewise performed well. She is starting her fifth car and no longer has to advertise to gain business. It continues to expand at a fast enough rate through word of mouth alone and has a much higher profile both locally and beyond, such that she has occasionally to decline work which is too far away to be economic for her. Diana says that, on balance, she too has no regrets about the franchise. The things that go wrong are caused by general business problems and are not problems with the franchise itself. Diana too cited staffing as being the main problem area in her business.

Janet Dunn was winner of the 1994 Franchisee of the Year Award for 'Achievement through Commitment'. Janet too has no regrets at all about having bought her South London-based Molly Maid franchise. She still firmly believes that franchising is a speedy way for women in particular to get into business. Her business doubled in the year of the Award and then consolidated, allowing her time to pursue other interests as well. Janet sold her business as a going concern in April 1996 and has since completed her studies for an MBA, moving into work which helps women entrepreneurs and women returners to become successful in their own careers.

The father and son partnership of Ronnie and Robbie Telfer still run their Interlink Express franchise at Trowbridge in Wiltshire. When contacted, Robbie was away on holiday, leaving his dad Ronnie minding the business. He reported that the business has grown by about 10 per cent since the first questionnaire, and that they have also taken over a further area since November 1996. The second area is one which had not been developed, but for which they have hopes for increased growth.

When a major customer moved from the area to set up in Milton Keynes, their original business had suffered a serious set-back, reducing their turnover by about 40 per cent. Even so, six years on from launch, retired bank manager Ronnie has no regrets about having bought the franchise, commenting that if he had not invested in it, he felt all his money would have just gone.

Greenalls Inn Partnership franchisee Nora Johnston had run the Travellers Rest public house in Runcorn, Lancashire, since August 1992. By the summer of 1996 Nora had quadrupled turnover at the pub and decided to realise it as a capital asset, selling it to her barman, Mark. Since that time Nora has enjoyed a well-earned break and is building on her Investors in People and training expertise to develop possible consultancy work. She has developed her own career by obtaining NVQ qualifications and is now an assessor for NVQs for the British Institute of Innkeeping, in which she remains the very active Secretary and Treasurer for the North West Region.

Award winners

The following details are supplied courtesy of John Burley Public Relations Consultants Ltd of Matlock who are the organisers of the British Franchise Association's awards, which are sponsored by Midland Bank and *The Express*. The competitions were only open to members of the British Franchise Association.

The finalists of the 1996 Franchisee of the Year competition were:

1st Prize Winner: Richard and Kim Bird, Bristol – City Link
2nd Prize Winner: Wilson Derbyshire, Northallerton & Newcastle-upon-Tyne – Saks
3rd Prize Winner: Jean and John Taylor, The Derby Arms, Inskip, Lancs – Greenalls
Finalists: Terry and Marcelle Woods, Chiswick, London – Kall Kwik
Sandra Redmond, Wimbledon, London – Molly Maid
Andrew Murdoch, Barking, Essex – Prontaprint
Huw Smith, Cardiff and Swansea – Rainbow International
Graham and Merryl Cornhill, East Anglia – Mobile Phone Centre
John and Julia Foad, Ashford, Kent – ServiceMaster

The winner of the 1997 Franchisor of the Year Award:

Pirtek (UK) Ltd – Specialist on-site hydraulic service
Finalists: Pirtek (UK) Ltd, Signs Express, Travail Employment Group Ltd, Saks Hair (Holdings) Ltd, Minster Services Group UK, MPC (Mobile Phone Centres), Stagecoach Theatre Arts.

The winner of the 1997 Newcomer of the Year Award:

Select Appointments Plc – Staffing services
Finalists: Select Appointments Plc – employment agency, Drinkmaster – beverage systems, Sevenoaks Franchising Ltd – specialist HiFi, video and home cinema retailers.

The winner of the 1997 Midland Bank Award:

Saks Hair (Holdings) Ltd

10

Sources of further information and advice

Whether your concern to find out more about franchising stems from your attraction to one particular company, or from an interest in franchising as a concept that may be applicable to your own self-employed future, the following sources of further information are available to you and should be used.

Inclusion of any organisation that is run commercially is not to be taken as a recommendation. Nor should the exclusion of a commercial organisation from the list be interpreted as an indication of criticism.

Chapter 2. What's in a name?

The British Franchise Association
Franchise Chambers,
Thames View
Newtown Road
Henley-on-Thames
Oxon RG9 1HG
Tel: 01491 578049/50
Fax: 01491 573517

The BFA is the professional association representing its franchisor members. It does not represent franchisees. However, it does supply a very useful information pack for prospective franchisees.

Business Franchise (magazine) A bi-monthly franchise journal, the official magazine of the BFA, available from all leading newsagents. *Business Franchise* also publish the annual *Business Franchise Handbook* directory.

Franchise World (magazine)
James House
37 Nottingham Road
London SW17 7EA
Tel: 0181 767 1371
Fax: 0181 767 2211

A bi-monthly franchise journal available only on subscription direct from the publishers, who also produce the annual *Franchise World Directory* and a range of books on franchising.

The Franchise Magazine, published five times a year. Available from leading newsagents.

Daily newspapers. These often carry features on franchising in their business pages. The *Daily Express* carries a regular feature on franchising every Monday.

Exhibitions. Regular exhibitions devoted solely to franchising are held throughout the year: the National Franchise Exhibition is organised by Blenheim and sponsored by the *Daily Express* at the NEC, Birmingham each autumn. The British Franchise Exhibition is organised by CII in London, Glasgow, Manchester and Dublin.

Business library. Your local business library may stock a selection of books covering the various aspects of franchising, and self-employment in general.

Further reading

Taking up a Franchise, Colin Barrow and Godfrey Golzen (Kogan Page, annual).
How to Evaluate a Franchise, Martin Mendelsohn (Franchise World, 1989).
Body and Soul, Anita Roddick. (Vermilion, 1992).
Franchising, A Guide for Franchisors and Franchisees, Iain Maitland (Mercury Business Paperbacks, 1991).

Chapter 3. Legal aspects

For guidance on forming a limited company, your local *Yellow Pages* will contain details of company registration agents in your area. Alternatively, take advice from your solicitor or accountant, or contact the Companies Registration Office direct:

For England and Wales:
Companies Registration Office
Companies House
Crown Way
Maindy
Cardiff CF4 3UZ
Tel: 01222 388588

For Scotland:
Companies Registration Office
100–102 George Street
Edinburgh EH2 3DJ
Tel: 0131 225 5774

A list of legal firms affiliated to the BFA can be obtained directly from the BFA. For a list of commercial solicitors in your area, contact

The Law Society:
The Law Society
50–52 Chancery Lane
London WC2A 1SX
Tel: 0171 242 1222

Further reading

Forming a Limited Company, Patricia Clayton, 4th edition (Kogan Page, 1994).

Chapter 4. Financial aspects

A list of qualified accountants in your area can be obtained from:

The Institute of Chartered Accountants in England and Wales
PO Box 433
Chartered Accountants Hall
Moorgate Place
London EC2P 2BJ
Tel: 0171 628 7060

The Institute of Chartered Accountants of Scotland
27 Queen Street
Edinburgh EH2 1LA
Tel: 0131 225 5673

Chartered Association of Certified Accountants
29 Lincoln's Inn Fields
London WC2A 3EE
Tel: 0171 242 6855

The following banks provide free information packs and advice on franchising through their local commercial branches: Barclays, Lloyds, Midland, National Westminster and the Royal Bank of Scotland.

Association of British Insurers
Aldermary House
10–15 Queen Street
London EC4N 1TT
Tel: 0171 248 4477

British Insurance and Investment Brokers Association
BIIBA House
14 Bevis Marks
London EC3A 7NT
Tel: 0171 623 9043

Department of Trade and Industry
Small Firms and Business Links Division
Level 2, St Mary's House
c/o Moorfoot
Sheffield S1 4PQ
Tel: 0114 2597325

Local Department of Trade and Industry (DTI) offices are listed in the telephone directory. The DTI has regional offices throughout the UK.

Local Investment Networking Company
LINC
4 Snow Hill
London EC1A 2BS
Tel: 0171 236 3000

Training and Enterprise Councils/Local Enterprise Companies. See your telephone directory for your local contact number and address.

Welsh Development Agency
Head Office
Pearl House
Greyfriars Road
Cardiff CF1 3XX
Tel: 01222 222666

Development Board for Rural Wales
Ladywell House
Newtown
Mid-Wales SY16 1JB
Tel: 01686 626965

Local Enterprise Development Unit
LEDU House
Upper Galwally
Belfast BT8 4TB
Tel: 01232 491031

Scottish Business Shops
(Headquarters)
120 Bothwell Street
Glasgow G2 7JP
Tel: 0141 248 6014; or Freephone 0800 787 878

Highlands and Islands Enterprise
Bridge House
20 Bridge Street
Inverness IV1 1QR
Tel: 01463 234171

Women's Enterprise Development Agency
31 Frederick Street
Hockley
Birmingham B1 3HH
Tel: 0121 236 2707

Women into Business
Suite 46
Westminster Palace Gardens
Artillery Row
London SW1P 1RR
Tel: 0171 976 7262/3

Small Firms Centre
2nd Floor
11 Belgrave Road
London SW1V 1RB
Tel: 0171 828 6271

Action for Cities
Tel: 0171 276 3890
This is a government sponsored programme run by the Department of the Environment.

Rural Development Commission Headquarters
141 Castle Street
Salisbury
Wiltshire SP1 3TP
Tel: 01722 336255

British Steel Industry Ltd
Canterbury House
2–6 Sydenham Road
Croydon
Surrey CR9 2LJ
Tel: 0181 686 2311

The Prince's Youth Business Trust
5th Floor
5 Cleveland Place
London SW1Y 6JJ
Tel: 0171 321 6500

Further reading

Financial Management for the Small Business, 3rd edition, Colin Barrow (Kogan Page, 1995).

Chapter 5. Your own closer look

To research any particular company, refer to the relevant Companies House (details given above). Your local business library may offer on-line facilities for a fee.

The London Search Room is located at:
55–71 City Road
London EC1Y 1BB
Tel: 0171 253 9393

Trade Marks Registry
Search and Advisory Service
The Patent Office
Hazlitt House

45 Southampton Buildings
Chancery Lane
London WC2A 1AR
Tel: 0171 438 7000

The register of trade marks and service marks may be inspected between 10am and 4pm, Monday to Friday, public holidays excepted. Copies of entries in the register can be supplied by the London Front Office on the above number.

On payment of the prescribed fee, anyone may search among the classified representations and indexes of trade and service marks at the Trade Marks Registry of the Patent Office. Online word mark searching can be carried out at the Newport, London and Manchester offices of the registry while device mark searches (hard copy) can only be carried out at Newport and London. The three main addresses of the Patent Office's Trade Mark Registry are:
Newport: Cardiff Road, Newport, Gwent NP9 1RH.
Manchester: Trade Marks Registry, Companies House, 75 Mosley Street Manchester M2 2HR.
London: As for the Search and Advisory Service above.

Chapter 6. Recruitment and selection

The Franchise (Information) Centre
Greenwood Business Centre
Goodiers Drive
Manchester M5 4QH
Tel: 0161 877 7788
Fax: 0161 877 5600

Further reading

For ideas about selling skills, see:

All About Selling, Alan Williams (McGraw-Hill, 1983).

How to Sell More – A Daily Express Guide for Small Business, Neil Johnson (Kogan Page, 1994)

Secrets of Telephone Selling, Neil Johnson, (Kogan Page, 1994).

Selling to Win, Richard Denny (Kogan Page, 1997).

Index

Index of Advertisers